HTML5: Basic

Student Manual

HTML5: Basic

CEO, Axzo Press: Ken Wasnock
Vice President, Content and Delivery: Josh Pincus
Director of Publishing Systems Development: Dan Quackenbush
Writer: Brandon Heffernan
Copyeditor: Catherine Oliver
Keytester: Cliff Coryea

For more information, go to www.logicaloperations.com

Trademarks

ILT Series is a trademark of Axzo Press.

Some of the product names and company names used in this book have been used for identification purposes only and may be trademarks or registered trademarks of their respective manufacturers and sellers.

Disclaimer

We reserve the right to revise this publication and make changes from time to time in its content without notice.

Student Manual
ISBN 10: 1-4260-2918-7
ISBN 13: 978-1-4260-2918-9

Printed in the United States of America

1 2 3 4 5 GL 06 05 04 03

Contents

Introduction

After reading this introduction, you will know how to:

A Use ILT Series manuals in general.

B Use prerequisites, a target student description, course objectives, and a skills inventory to properly set your expectations for the course.

C Re-key this course after class.

Topic A: About the manual

ILT Series philosophy

Our manuals facilitate your learning by providing structured interaction with the software itself. While we provide text to explain difficult concepts, the hands-on activities are the focus of our courses. By paying close attention as your instructor leads you through these activities, you will learn the skills and concepts effectively.

We believe strongly in the instructor-led class. During class, focus on your instructor. Our manuals are designed and written to facilitate your interaction with your instructor, and not to call attention to manuals themselves.

We believe in the basic approach of setting expectations, delivering instruction, and providing summary and review afterwards. For this reason, lessons begin with objectives and end with summaries. We also provide overall course objectives and a course summary to provide both an introduction to and closure on the entire course.

Manual components

The manuals contain these major components:

- Table of contents
- Introduction
- Units
- Course summary
- Glossary
- Index

Each element is described below.

Table of contents

The table of contents acts as a learning roadmap.

Introduction

The introduction contains information about our training philosophy and our manual components, features, and conventions. It contains target student, prerequisite, objective, and setup information for the specific course.

Units

Units are the largest structural component of the course content. A unit begins with a title page that lists objectives for each major subdivision, or topic, within the unit. Within each topic, conceptual and explanatory information alternates with hands-on activities. Units conclude with a summary comprising one paragraph for each topic, and an independent practice activity that gives you an opportunity to practice the skills you've learned.

The conceptual information takes the form of text paragraphs, exhibits, lists, and tables. The activities are structured in two columns, one telling you what to do, the other providing explanations, descriptions, and graphics.

Course summary

This section provides a text summary of the entire course. It is useful for providing closure at the end of the course. The course summary also indicates the next course in this series, if there is one, and lists additional resources you might find useful as you continue to learn about the software.

Glossary

The glossary provides definitions for all of the key terms used in this course.

Index

The index at the end of this manual makes it easy for you to find information about a particular software component, feature, or concept.

Manual conventions

We've tried to keep the number of elements and the types of formatting to a minimum in the manuals. This aids in clarity and makes the manuals more classically elegant looking. But there are some conventions and icons you should know about.

Item	Description
Italic text	In conceptual text, indicates a new term or feature.
Bold text	In unit summaries, indicates a key term or concept. In an independent practice activity, indicates an explicit item that you select, choose, or type.
`Code font`	Indicates code or syntax.

`Longer strings of ▶`
`code will look ▶`
`like this.`
	In the hands-on activities, any code that's too long to fit on a single line is divided into segments by one or more continuation characters (▶). This code should be entered as a continuous string of text.

Select **bold item**	In the left column of hands-on activities, bold sans-serif text indicates an explicit item that you select, choose, or type.
Keycaps like ↵ ENTER	Indicate a key on the keyboard you must press.

Hands-on activities

The hands-on activities are the most important parts of our manuals. They are divided into two primary columns. The "Here's how" column gives short instructions to you about what to do. The "Here's why" column provides explanations, graphics, and clarifications. Here's a sample:

Do it!

A-1: Creating a commission formula

Here's how	Here's why
1 Open Sales	This is an oversimplified sales compensation worksheet. It shows sales totals, commissions, and incentives for five sales reps.
2 Observe the contents of cell F4	F4 = =E4*C_Rate The commission rate formulas use the name "C_Rate" instead of a value for the commission rate.

For these activities, we have provided a collection of data files designed to help you learn each skill in a real-world business context. As you work through the activities, you will modify and update these files. Of course, you might make a mistake and therefore want to re-key the activity starting from scratch. To make it easy to start over, you will rename each data file at the end of the first activity in which the file is modified. Our convention for renaming files is to add the word "My" to the beginning of the file name. In the above activity, for example, a file called "Sales" is being used for the first time. At the end of this activity, you would save the file as "My sales," thus leaving the "Sales" file unchanged. If you make a mistake, you can start over using the original "Sales" file.

In some activities, however, it might not be practical to rename the data file. If you want to retry one of these activities, ask your instructor for a fresh copy of the original data file.

Topic B: Setting your expectations

Properly setting your expectations is essential to your success. This topic will help you do that by providing:

- Prerequisites for this course
- A description of the target student
- A list of the objectives for the course
- A skills assessment for the course

Course prerequisites

Before taking this course, you should be familiar with personal computers and the use of a keyboard and a mouse. You should also be familiar with the Internet and have experience with using a browser to view Web pages. Furthermore, this course assumes that you've completed the following course or have equivalent experience:

- *Windows 7: Basic, Windows Vista: Basic,* or *Windows XP: Basic*

Target student

You will get the most out of this course if you're new to Web development and you want to learn how to use HTML and CSS to create Web pages. Even if you're already familiar with previous versions of HTML, you can benefit by learning about some of the new elements of HTML5.

Course objectives

These overall course objectives will give you an idea about what to expect from the course. It is also possible that they will help you see that this course is not the right one for you. If you think you either lack the prerequisite knowledge or already know most of the subject matter to be covered, you should let your instructor know that you think you are misplaced in the class.

After completing this course, you will know how to:

- Create an HTML document from scratch; identify basic HTML syntax; create well-formed code; declare an HTML5 document; and define a basic document structure that includes headings and paragraphs.
- Create a semantically meaningful document structure by using several new HTML5 elements; create lists; apply a variety of phrase elements; insert character entities; and modify elements by using various attributes.
- Embed a style sheet and write basic CSS rules to format HTML content; create an external style sheet and link documents to it; apply color, text, and font styles; apply borders, margins, and padding; control element dimensions; create both fixed and flexible widths; and apply styles using IDs.
- Create and modify tables to display tabular data; define a table structure, including headers, the table body, and a footer; apply styles to table elements; and span rows and columns to arrange data, headers, and footers.
- Create links to internal and external resources; apply styles to various link states; apply styles to elements based on their context in the document structure; identify various image formats; embed an image and provide an effective text alternative; and apply background images from a style sheet.

Skills inventory

Use the following form to gauge your skill level entering the class. For each skill listed, rate your familiarity from 1 to 5, with five being the most familiar. *This is not a test.* Rather, it is intended to provide you with an idea of where you're starting from at the beginning of class. If you're wholly unfamiliar with all the skills, you might not be ready for the class. If you think you already understand all of the skills, you might need to move on to the next course in the series. In either case, you should let your instructor know as soon as possible.

Skill	1	2	3	4	5
Identifying basic HTML syntax					
Identifying advantages of HTML5					
Creating a basic HTML document from scratch					
Creating well-formed code					
Declaring a document as HTML5					
Defining headings and paragraphs					
Creating a semantically meaningful document structure					
Applying the <header> element					
Applying the <section> element					
Applying the <nav> element					
Applying the <footer> element					
Creating ordered and unordered lists					
Applying phrase elements, including <em>, <strong>, and <cite>					
Inserting character entities					
Applying attributes to elements					
Declaring a document's primary language					
Applying IDs to augment a document structure					
Defining quotations and their sources					
Embedding a style sheet					
Writing CSS rules					
Creating an external style sheet					
Linking HTML documents to an external style sheet					

Skill	1	2	3	4	5
Applying color and background color					
Setting an element's font and font size					
Controlling line height and text alignment					
Controlling letter spacing					
Applying CSS borders					
Controlling margins					
Applying padding					
Creating box shadows and rounded corners					
Creating both fixed and flexible widths					
Controlling element dimensions					
Applying styles to an ID					
Creating tables					
Applying the <thead>, <tbody>, and <tfoot> elements					
Applying styles to table elements					
Spanning rows and columns to arrange data, headers, and footers					
Creating internal and external links					
Making a link open in a new browser window or tab					
Applying styles to link states					
Applying styles to elements based on their context					
Identifying the differences between the GIF, JPG, and PNG formats					
Embedding an image					
Writing effective text alternatives for embedded images					
Applying background images from a style sheet					

Topic C: Re-keying the course

If you have the proper hardware and software, you can re-key this course after class. This section explains what you'll need in order to do so, and how to do it.

Hardware requirements

Your personal computer should have:

- A keyboard and a mouse
- A 500 MHz processor (or faster)
- At least 256 MB RAM
- At least 1.5 GB of available hard disk space
- An SVGA monitor (1024×768 or higher resolution)

Software requirements

You will also need the following software:

- Windows 7, Windows XP, or Windows Vista, updated with the most recent service packs

  Note: This course was written for Windows 7.
- Firefox 4 or later

Network requirements

The following network components and connectivity are also required for re-keying this course:

- Internet access, for the following purposes:
  - Downloading the latest critical updates and service packs
  - Completing activity A-2 in the unit titled "Links and images"

Setup instructions to re-key the course

Before you re-key the course, you will need to perform the following steps.

1 Use Windows Update to install all available critical updates and Service Packs.

2 With flat-panel displays, we recommend using the panel's native resolution for best results. Color depth/quality should be set to High (24 bit) or higher.

   Please note that your display settings or resolution may differ from the author's, so your screens might not exactly match the screenshots in this manual.

3 Configure Windows Explorer to display file extensions as follows:

   a Open Windows Explorer.

   b Choose Organize, Folder and Search Options.

   c On the View tab, clear Hide extensions for known file types, and click OK.

4 If you have the data disc that came with this manual, locate the Student Data folder on it and copy it to the desktop of your computer.

   If you don't have the data disc, you can download the Student Data files for the course:

   a Connect to http://downloads.logicaloperations.com.
   b Enter the course title or search by part to locate this course
   c Click the course title to display a list of available downloads.
   Note: Data Files are located under the Instructor Edition of the course.
   d Click the link(s) for downloading the Student Data files.
   e Create a folder named Student Data on the desktop of your computer.
   f Double-click the downloaded zip file(s) and drag the contents into the Student Data folder.

Unit 1
Getting started

Unit time: 40 minutes

Complete this unit, and you'll know how to:

A Identify the advantages of using HTML5 and some of its features, and describe basic HTML syntax and authoring guidelines.

B Create a simple Web page with a basic document structure, and define headings and paragraphs.

Topic A: Introduction to HTML5

Explanation

HTML5 builds on its predecessor, version 4, and introduces several new elements and attributes. HTML5 enables and encourages semantically meaningful markup and rich Web applications. Before you get started writing HTML5 code, a little history will likely prove helpful.

A brief history of HTML and XHTML

Web pages are built with HTML, which stands for *Hypertext Markup Language*. An HTML document is a text file that contains elements, or *tags*, that tell a browser how to display its content. You can create HTML documents with any text editor, such as Notepad on a Windows computer or TextEdit on the Macintosh. HTML documents have an .html or .htm extension, as in mypage.html.

HTML5 is the last of several versions of HTML that started with version 1.0. After version 4, *XHTML* (Extensible Hypertext Markup Language) emerged as a stricter implementation of Web page markup, with authoring rules intended to make Web content more interoperable, streamlined, and cleanly structured.

As with XHTML, valid HTML5 documents must be free of any style-related elements and attributes. All formatting information must separated from the document structure by using a style sheet; this separation results in code that is lean, loads quickly, is easy to modify, and produces pages that are displayed consistently on a variety of platforms and devices.

Going forward, standards bodies intend to drop the numeric versioning and refer to it simply as HTML, a living standard that evolves and expands over time.

Advantages of HTML5

HTML5 expands on the previous version and enables many new features and techniques. Following are some key advantages of using HTML5:

- It's easier to stream video and music. New elements in HTML5 have allowed modern browsers to provide built-in functionality, eliminating the need for plug-ins such as Flash and Silverlight.
- New elements help make the page structure more meaningful. Elements such as `<section>`, `<header>`, and `<footer>` allow you to create more semantically meaningful document structures.
- Content is more accessible to alternative devices. Several new elements and attributes enable improved functionality for users of such devices as Braille printers and screen readers.
- HTML5 provides new advanced capabilities for Web application developers. This new functionality for rich Web applications includes a local database API (application programming interface), geolocation, and enhanced forms.

Do it!

A-1: Discussing HTML5

Questions	Answers
1 What is an HTML document?	
2 How can you create an HTML document?	
3 Briefly describe two advantages of using HTML5	
4 Why must formatting information be separate from the HTML code?	

HTML5 syntax and authoring guidelines

Explanation

The syntax for HTML5 is the same as for previous versions. HTML5 consists of predefined elements, also referred to as *tags*, which define the structure of a Web document. All elements are set in angle brackets (< and >). For example, to start an HTML document structure, you insert an `<html>` tag at the top of the file.

Most HTML elements are containers, meaning that they are meant to contain content for display and other HTML elements. Container tags have an opening tag and a closing tag. For example, the following line is defined as a paragraph by the opening `<p>` tag and the corresponding closing `</p>` tag:

```
<p> This text is defined as a paragraph. </p>
```

All closing tags use the forward slash (/) to define the end of an element.

Authoring guidelines

HTML5 is not considered strict in terms of authoring requirements. For example, you can write tags and attributes in uppercase or lowercase. However, it's arguably best to follow the guidelines of XHTML, which are as follows:

- Write element names and attributes in lowercase letters.
- Container tags must have corresponding closing tags.
- Put attribute values in quotation marks.
- Make sure your HTML code structure is well-formed.

The benefits of following these authoring guidelines include:

- Your content will be displayed consistently in a variety of browsers and devices, including smart phones.
- Your content will be reliably accessible to site visitors who use alternative devices such as Braille printers and screen readers
- Adhering to a set of authoring rules will make it easier to collaborate with other developers.
- Consistent code results in fewer mistakes and easier maintenance.
- You can build Web applications that work with XML.

Well-formed code

In a *well-formed* code structure, all elements are properly nested. *Nesting* refers to the parent-child relationships of elements in a document. For example, in the following code, the `<em>` element is nested inside a `<p>` element, making that `<em>` element a child of that paragraph. In other words, the `<p>` element is a parent of the `<em>` element.

```
<p>This is a paragraph with an emphasized <em>word</em>.</p>
```

The order in which nested elements are closed is critical to creating well-formed code. A simple phrase to remember is "first to open, last to close." Exhibit 1-1 shows an example of invalid code nesting:

```
<p>This paragraph has some <em> emphasized text </p>.</em>
```

Exhibit 1-1: Invalid code nesting

Exhibit 1-2 shows the same code properly nested. Note that the brackets that indicate the beginning and end of the elements do not overlap.

```
<p>This paragraph has some <em> emphasized text </em>.</p>
```

Exhibit 1-2: Proper code nesting

These are simple examples that might seem obvious, but in larger documents that contain multiple layers of nested elements, it's sometimes easy to lose track of the nesting order. Many HTML authoring tools provide visual indicators whenever code is improperly nested. If you use a simple text editor, however, it's especially important to pay close attention to how your HTML tags are nested in the document hierarchy.

Do it!

A-2: Discussing HTML syntax and best practices

Questions and answers

1 What is a container tag?

2 Describe some benefits of using the authoring rules of XHTML

3 Which of the following represents well-formed code?

A `<p>Is it <em>this example</p></em>?`

B `<p>Or is it <em>this example</em></p>?`

C `<p>Or maybe <em>this example</p>?`

4 A simple phrase that can help you create well-formed code is:

A First to open, first to close

B Last to open, last to close

C First to open, last to close

5 Which of the following is true given a paragraph element that contains an `<em>` tag to specify emphasis for a word or phrase?

A The `<em>` tag is a sibling of the paragraph.

B The `<em>` tag is a child of the paragraph; the `<p>` tag is therefore its parent element.

C The `<p>` tag is both a parent and sibling of the `<em>` tag.

Topic B: Basic HTML structure

Explanation

While HTML5 introduces many new elements and attributes, the basic core structural elements are the same as they were in version 4. You will start by defining the document type, and then you'll add a head, a title, and a document body. Then you'll define headings and paragraphs.

The Document type declaration

The *doctype* (document type) declaration must be the first thing that appears in an HTML document; it defines the document type. In previous versions of HTML, the doctype declaration was long and difficult to remember. In HTML5, the doctype declaration is simplified, and you don't need to include the `5` after `html` in the statement. To define the document as an HTML5 document, add the following code to the top of your page:

```
<!DOCTYPE html>
```

Including this doctype declaration is critical because it tells the browser what kind of markup is used, and this information affects how the browser displays the page. The declaration above tells the browser that the document is HTML5 to ensure proper rendering of the new HTML5 elements and features.

Many Web authoring tools, such as Microsoft's Expression Web and Adobe's Dreamweaver, automatically insert a doctype declaration based on settings you choose.

Basic structure

HTML documents must have three basic structural elements: `<html>`, `<head>`, and `<body>`. These elements establish the framework for a Web page.

Element	Description
`<html> </html>`	An HTML document's root element. All other HTML tags are contained in this element.
`<head> </head>`	Contains information *about* the document. This information is not part of the page's body. Head elements include the page title and links to resources such as style sheets and scripts.
`<body> </body>`	Contains the page's content, including all display elements and text content.

A minimal HTML document will look something like this:

```
<!DOCTYPE html>
<html>
<head>
  <title>My Document</title>
</head>
<body>
This is the page content.
</body>
</html>
```

The <title> element

The `<title>` element is valid only inside the `<head>` element. The text inside the `<title>` element appears in the browser's title bar, at the top of the browser window. The title is not displayed as text on the page. When a user bookmarks your page, the text in the `<title>` element is used as the bookmark title, so it's important that you write titles that are both descriptive and concise.

Do it!

B-1: Creating a simple Web page

Here's how	Here's why
1 Open Windows Notepad	(In Windows 7, click Start, type *notepad*, and press Enter.) To open a new, blank text file.
2 Type the following code: `<!DOCTYPE html>`	To establish the page as an HTML5 document.
3 Press ENTER	To go to the next line.

Type the following code:
 	
`<html>`
`<head>`
`<title>My First Page</title>`
`</head>`
`<body>`
 	
`</body>`
`</html>`
	To set up the document's basic structure.

4 Save the file as **mypage.html**	(In the current topic folder.) To save the file as a Web page.
5 In Windows, navigate to the current topic folder	(In the Student Data folder on the desktop.) You'll open your new page in Firefox.
Right-click **mypage.html**	
Choose **Open with**, **Firefox**	To open the page in Firefox. The page is blank except for the title, which is displayed in the browser's title bar. To add content to this page, you need to add text or other elements inside the `<body>` element.
6 Switch to Notepad	
Inside the <body> container, type your name	
Press CTRL + S	To save your changes. You can also choose File, Save.
7 In Firefox, click [reload button]	To reload the page and view your changes.

8 Switch to Notepad	
Click after your name and press ENTER	To create a new line in the HTML file.
Type more text	Such as your address or today's date.
Save your changes	Press Ctrl + S, or choose File, Save.
9 Switch to Firefox and press F5	To reload the page. Your name and the additional text appear as one line of text, even though you entered a line break in the file. This occurs because line breaks must be created with HTML tags. Using paragraph tags is one way to do this.
10 Close Firefox	
Close Notepad	

Headings

Explanation

Headings are one of the most basic content elements. There are six heading levels in HTML: <h1> through <h6>. They're all meant to define the logical progression of headings and subheadings in a document hierarchy. To define a level-one heading, you'd write:

```
<h1>Heading Text</h1>
```

Browsers apply default styles to heading elements in order to visually indicate their place in the document structure. Browsers display headings as bold text at varying font sizes, as shown in Exhibit 1-3.

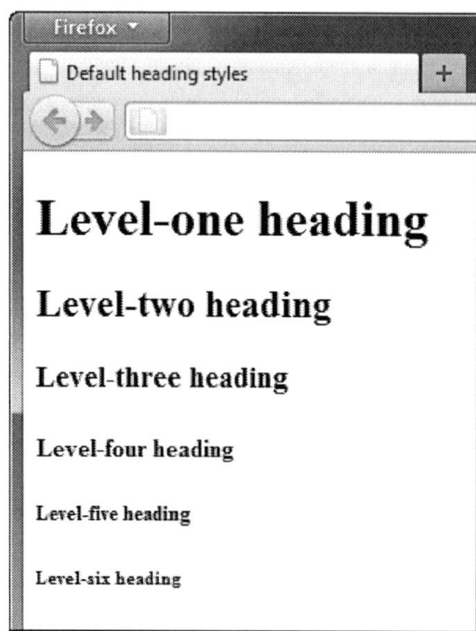

Exhibit 1-3: Default heading styles

Paragraphs: The <p> element

Use the <p> element when you want to define a block of text as a paragraph. The <p> element creates line breaks above and below the paragraph content. For example, the following paragraph is contained in a <p> element:

```
<p>
This is paragraph text. It starts with the opening tag and
ends with the closing tag. This text will have line breaks
above and below it.
</p>
```

Exhibit 1-4 shows a page with two levels of headings and two paragraphs. Exhibit 1-5 shows the HTML code for the page.

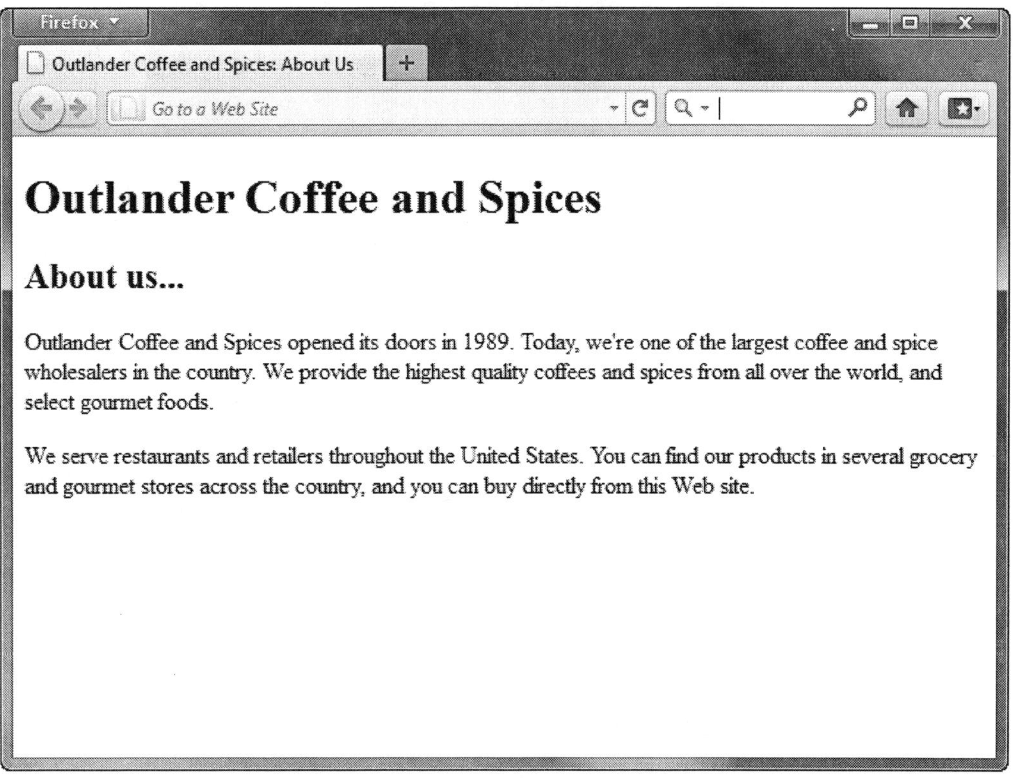

Exhibit 1-4: The about.html page after the activity

```
<!DOCTYPE html>
<html>
<head>
  <title>Outlander Coffee and Spices: About Us</title>
</head>

<body>

<h1>Outlander Coffee and Spices</h1>

<h2>About us...</h2>

<p>
Outlander Coffee and Spices opened its doors in 1989. Today, we're one of
the largest coffee and spice wholesalers in the country. We provide the highest
quality coffees and spices from all over the world, and select gourmet foods.
</p>

<p>
We serve restaurants and retailers throughout the United States. You can find
our products in several grocery and gourmet stores across the country, and you
can buy directly from this Web site.
</p>

</body>
</html>
```

Exhibit 1-5: The HTML code for the page shown in Exhibit 1-4.

Do it!

B-2: Defining headings and paragraphs

The files for this activity are in Student Data folder **Unit 1\Topic B**.

Here's how	Here's why
1 Start Notepad	
Choose **File**, **Open**	
Navigate to the **Student Data** folder and then to the current topic folder	The Student Data folder is on the desktop.
2 At the bottom of the dialog box, click **Text Documents**	
Choose **All Files**	To view all file types.
Double-click **about.html**	To open it in Notepad. This file contains text inside a `<body>` container. You'll apply HTML elements to define the structure of this content.
Enable Word Wrap in Notepad	(If necessary.) Select Format, Word Wrap.
3 In Firefox, open about.html	The text is not formatted with any HTML tags, so it appears as a single block.
4 Add the following bold code around the text shown: `<h1>Outlander Coffee and Spices</h1>`	
5 Save your changes	Press Ctrl + S.
6 Switch to Firefox and reload the page	(Click the Reload button or press F5.) To view the result. The text is now defined as a level-one heading, so it appears on its own line in large, bold type.
7 Add the following bold code around the text shown: `<h2>About us...</h2>`	
8 Save your changes and reload the page in Firefox	To view the result. The text is now defined as a level-two heading, so it appears on its own line in bold text that's larger than default text but smaller than the level-one heading.
9 Wrap the remaining two text blocks in separate `<p>` elements	(Refer to Exhibit 1-5.) To create two paragraphs.

10 Save your changes and reload the page in Firefox	To view the result. Your page should look like Exhibit 1-4.
11 Close Firefox and Notepad	

Unit summary: Getting started

Topic A

In this topic, you learned that **HTML** is composed of elements (“tags”) that tell a browser how to display content. You learned that **HTML5** expands on the previous version and supports the use of styles and scripts to enable new features and techniques. You learned about some **advantages** of HTML5, basic HTML syntax, and **authoring guidelines** to help ensure that your code is efficient and well-formed.

Topic B

In this topic, you learned how to create a simple Web page from scratch. You learned about the **document type declaration** and the basic document **structure**, including the <html>, <head>, and <body> tags. Finally, you learned how to define headings and paragraphs.

Independent practice activity

In this activity, you will add a document type declaration, define a basic HTML structure, and define headings and paragraphs.

The files for this activity are in Student Data folder **Unit 1\Unit summary**.

1 In Firefox, open about-us.html. (*Hint:* Navigate to the Unit summary folder and double-click about.html.)

2 In Notepad, open about-us.html.

3 At the top of the file, insert the doctype declaration for HTML5.

4 On the next line, insert an <html> tag.

5 Create a head container.

6 In the head section, add a <title> element that reads **About Us**.

7 Wrap the page content in a <body> container.

8 Make the text **Garage D’Or Books** a level-one heading.

9 Make the text **About us** and **Why we’re different** separate level-two headings.

10 Define the remaining text as three paragraphs. Make sure the <body> and <html> tags are closed at the bottom of the document, in that order. The completed code should look like Exhibit 1-6.

11 Save your changes and reload the page in Firefox. The page should look like Exhibit 1-7.

```
<!DOCTYPE html>
<html>
<head>
<title>About Us</title>
</head>

<body>

<h1>Garage D'or Books</h1>

<h2>About us</h2>

<p>In French, d'or means "of gold". If you are a lover of antique, rare, and
out-of-print books, our "garage of gold" is sure to delight. </p>

<p>We opened the Garage in 2000 as an alternative to the mostly modern and
commercial book sellers that are available online. Today, thanks to many great
relationships with small publishers and collectors worldwide, we have an
inventory of antique, academic, and otherwise rare and out-of-print books that
we believe is unmatched anywhere. </p>

<h2>Why we're different</h2>

<p>Unlike other popular online book sellers, we won't inundate you with
advertising and unnecessary features. We prefer that you feel as though you're
at a corner bookstore, with an old-world aesthetic and library atmosphere. We
are building a community, and we welcome you not only as a customer, but as a
potential partner. If you have access to antique, rare, or out-of-print books,
you can sell them through us. </p>

</body>
</html>
```

Exhibit 1-6: The completed HTML

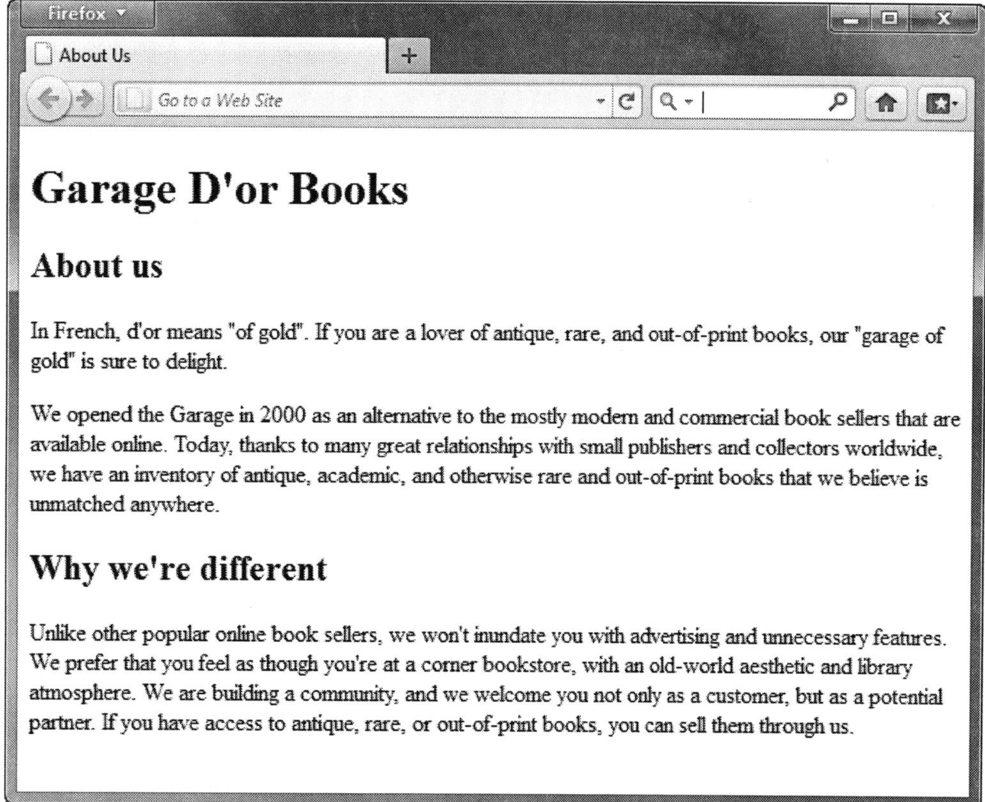

Exhibit 1-7: The completed page, viewed in Firefox

Unit 2

Elements and attributes

Unit time: 75 minutes

Complete this unit, and you'll know how to:

A Create semantically meaningful document structures.

B Apply phrase elements to logically define text content.

C Apply attributes and mark up quotes and abbreviations.

Topic A: Document structure

Explanation

In addition to the many structural elements carried over from previous versions, HTML5 introduces several new structural elements that you can use to create more semantically meaningful markup than previous versions of HTML could provide.

Semantically meaningful elements

Semantically meaningful elements are those elements that are self-descriptive; they describe the purpose of the content they contain. For example, a `<section>` element defines a document section, and a `<footer>` element defines the footer content for a document or section. In previous versions of HTML, the generic `<div>` element was often used to define various document sections. While the `<div>` tag is still a valid and important element in HTML5, the lack of semantically meaningful structural elements in prior versions of HTML often led to a big mess of nested `<div>` tags on each page.

The new elements in HTML5 allow you to clarify your document structure and define its content more meaningfully. This in turn allows search engines and other Web applications to interact with your pages more effectively.

The <header> element

You can use the `<header>` element to define your document headers, such as the main page header or specific section headers. In other words, this element is intended to define not only top-level page information—such as a logo, slogan, or top-level heading—but also individual sections that require headings.

The `<header>` element does not replace the `<h1>` through `<h6>` tags—you can use them together to establish a page's or section's heading structure. The `<header>` tag provides a containing structure for a header and any related information you want to include in the header, such as a publication date. For example:

```
<header>
     <h1>Our Expansion Plan</h1>
     <p>Last updated on 12/22/12</p>
</header>
```

A `<header>` cannot contain another `<header>` element or a `<footer>` element.

The <hgroup> element

The `<hgroup>` element provides a containing structure for multiple consecutive headings (`<h1>` through `<h6>` elements), such as a top-level heading and a subheading. For example, if you have a page header that contains a company name and its slogan, you might define both items as one heading group, as follows:

```
<hgroup>
     <h1>Garage D'Or Books</h1>
     <h2>The Dear and Discounted</h2>
</hgroup>
```

You can use the <header> and <hgroup> elements together to define a more complex header structure. For example:

```
<header>
   <hgroup>
      <h1>Outlander Spices</h1>
      <h2>Our Expansion Plan</h2>
   </hgroup>
   <p>Last updated 12/22/12</p>
</header>
```

Do it!

A-1: Defining headers

The files for this activity are in Student Data folder **Unit 2\Topic A**.

Here's how	Here's why
1 In Windows Explorer, open the Student Data folder	On the desktop.
Open the current topic folder	In the current unit folder.
2 Double-click **news.html**	To open it in Firefox. The page has a basic structure with headings and paragraphs.
3 In Windows Explorer, right-click **news.html**	
Choose **Open with**, **Notepad**	To open the HTML file in Notepad. (If the command is not available, start Notepad, choose File, Open, and browse to open the file.)
4 Observe the date information	(In the first paragraph.) This information can be defined as part of the "Company news" heading structure.
5 Add the following bold code: **<header>** <h2>Company news</h2> <p>Last updated 12/22/12</p> **</header>**	To define a header that contains a level-two heading and date information.
6 Locate the other <h2> element	Scroll down, if necessary.
7 Add the following bold code: **<header>** <h2>A note about our history and future</h2> <p>By Alan Garver, President</p> **</header>**	To define a header that contains a level-two heading and date information.
8 Press CTRL + S	To save your changes. You can also choose File, Save.
9 What's the difference between the <header> and <hgroup> elements?	

10 True or false? All `<h1>` through `<h6>` elements should have a `<header>` tag as a parent element.

The <section> element

Explanation

The <section> element is meant to define document sections or application sections. Use it to group content into logical and distinct sections, like chapters in a story. For example, you might divide your Web site's home page into separate sections for the organization's history, news, and partners. Or you might organize product offerings into distinct sections, as follows:

```
<header>
     <h1>Outlander Coffee</h1>
     <p>(All options are available in decaf.)</p>
</header>
<section>
     <h1>Organic Coffee</h1>
     <p>Columbian</p>
     <p>Sumatran</p>
     <p>Hawaiian</p>
</section>
<section>
     <h1>Blends</h1>
     <p>Outlander Blend</p>
     <p>Pacific Blend</p>
     <p>African Blend</p>
</section>
```

Section headings

Each section should have its own heading. When defining a section, ask yourself what its heading should be. If a heading does not seem appropriate, then using a <section> element is probably not appropriate, either. In such a case, use whatever element best describes the content, or use the generic <div> element to define the section if no semantically meaningful element is suitable.

As shown in the preceding example, the <section> element allows for the use of multiple <h1> elements if the situation calls for it. The first heading is the document's top-level heading (the *root* heading), and the other two are the sections' top-level headings. The ability to give each section an independent heading structure is an important advancement in HTML5 because it allows applications that assemble Web pages on the fly to insert sections of independent content that automatically fit within the heading structure of the assembled page.

You can insert <section> elements inside other <section> elements as needed to establish a document outline that reflects the hierarchy of your information.

Indenting your code

In the previous code sample, the headings and paragraphs are indented under their parent element. Indenting your code in this way, or any way that suits your style, can help make your code easy to read and modify. Many HTML authoring programs, such as Dreamweaver, automatically indent elements under their parent element. Basic text editors like Notepad do not, so you'll need to use the Tab key or Spacebar if you want to indent certain elements to help clarify the document structure.

The <nav> element

The `<nav>` element is meant to define a page's navigation section, which contains links to other pages and resources in the Web site. Not all links on a page should be placed inside a `<nav>` container; use it only to contain the site's primary navigation options or links to specific sections of the page itself.

In addition to providing a structure for navigation links, the `<nav>` element also allows users of alternative browsing devices, such as screen readers, to easily skip over navigational information and go directly to page content.

The <footer> element

Use the `<footer>` element to define a page's footer content or the footer content of a specific document section. For example, a section footer might contain the author and date of an article or links to section references, while a page footer might contain copyright information, as shown in the following example:

```
<footer>
     Content © 2010 - 2015 Outlander Spices.
</footer>
```

A `<footer>` cannot contain another `<footer>` element or a `<header>` element.

A typical document structure

Putting these new structural elements together, we can create a page layout that looks something like Exhibit 2-1 (after applying layout styles to arrange the elements).

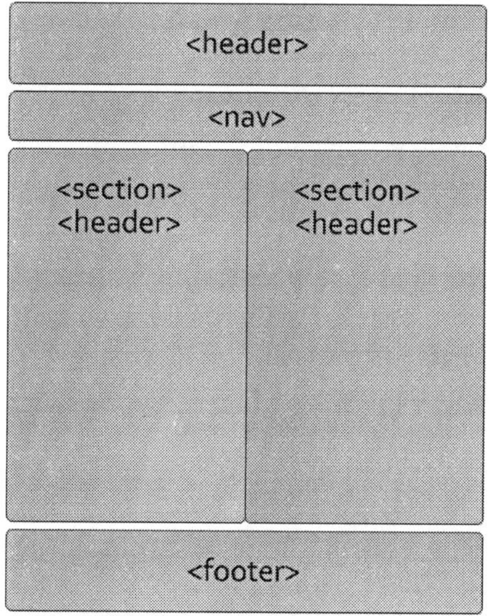

Exhibit 2-1: A typical page structure and layout

The <article> element

The `<article>` element defines a section of content intended to be used or distributed independently of other content. For example, a blog entry or syndicated article is best defined by the `<article>` element.

Articles can contain other `<article>` elements if the child articles are topically or thematically related to the parent article. For example, a syndicated blog entry would be the parent article, with user comments defined by individual `<article>` elements nested inside the parent article.

Advantages of creating well-structured documents

When you begin to establish the framework of a Web page, think of it as a traditional outline, and structure it accordingly. Consider how best to define the content you're working with and the hierarchy of the information. If text is a heading or subheading, define it as such. If it's a navigation section, define it as such.

There are many advantages of using HTML tags to describe the content they contain and to create a well-structured document outline. These advantages include the following:

- **Your pages will be easier to update and maintain.** The more efficient your code, the easier it is to make content and design changes. This can result in significant savings in human resources and maintenance costs. Other developers will be able to more easily read and understand your page structure.
- **It will be easier to incorporate your pages into application environments.** Web applications might be able to incorporate your content more effectively.
- **Search applications can index logically defined content more effectively.** Semantic markup helps some search engines determine the relevance of your content during a search.
- **Your pages will be forward-compatible and accessible.** Smart phones, screen readers, and many other devices of the present and future will be able to access your content efficiently.
- **Your pages will tend to load faster and more consistently.** The more efficient the code, the smaller the file size. Smaller file sizes result in significant savings in bandwidth and maintenance costs and produce a faster and more consistent browsing experience for your users.

Do it!

A-2: Defining document sections

Here's how	Here's why
1 Directly below the `<body>` element, type the following:	Between the `<body>` element and the `<h1>` element.
`<nav>Home | About | News | Products | Contact</nav>`	
	To define a navigation section. You will create navigation links later in the course.
2 Below the top heading, enter the following bold code:	To start a section.
`<h1>Outlander Coffee and Spices</h1>` **`<section>`**	
3 Close the section above the second header	After the paragraph that begins, "Outlander Spices is now ISO 9000 certified…."
4 Observe the second header and its content	This content can stand alone as an independent article, so you'll define it as such.
5 After the closing section tag, type the following: `<article>`	
6 Directly above the closing body tag, close the article	To define the note from Alan Garver as an article that can be used independently of the other page content.
7 After the closing article tag, type the following:	To create a separate news archive section.

`<section>`
`<h2>News archive</h2>`
`<p>January - June 2012</p>`
`<p>July - December 2011</p>`
`<p>January - June 2011</p>`
`</section>`	

8 Save your changes	Press Ctrl+S.
9 In Firefox, reload the page	(Click the Reload button or press F5.) To view your changes.
Observe the headings	Browsers apply default formatting to headings to help indicate the document's structure.
10 Switch to Notepad	

11 Why is it not necessary to use the <header> element in the "News archive" section?

12 After the last section, enter the following code and text:

(Directly above the closing body tag.) To create a page footer.

```
<footer>
Contents copyright 2011 - 2020 Outlander Spices
</footer>
```

13 Save your changes and reload the page in Firefox

Only the headings are given default formatting.

14 How might you use the <article> element in your own work?

15 True or false? A document's top-level, or root, heading should not be defined with an <h2> element.

16 How might well-structured, semantically meaningful documents benefit your own Web site?

Lists

Explanation

Structuring text into a list is often the best way to display certain types of information. There are three types of lists: unordered, ordered, and definition. An unordered list works well for items of equal importance, while an ordered list is best for items of varying importance or that follow a specific sequence. Use definition lists for terms and their definitions.

Unordered lists

Unordered lists create a series of bulleted items. You create an unordered list by using the <ul> and <li> elements. The <ul> (unordered list) element defines a series of items as an unordered list; each list item it contains will appear with a bullet character as its label. The <li> (list item) tag indicates a distinct item in the list. There is no limit to the number of items you can include in a list.

The following code will produce the result shown in Exhibit 2-2.

```
<h2>Stuffing ingredients:</h2>
<ul>
 <li>Cooked potatoes: 4 oz. </li>
 <li>Cooked cauliflower: 2 oz.</li>
 <li>Outlander parsley: 2 tsp</li>
 <li>Outlander dill seed: 1 tsp</li>
 <li>Mayonnaise: 1 tbsp</li>
 <li>Lemon juice: 1 tsp</li>
</ul>
```

Stuffing ingredients:

- Cooked potatoes: 4 oz.
- Cooked cauliflower: 2 oz.
- Outlander parsley: 2 tsp
- Outlander dill seed: 1 tsp
- Mayonnaise: 1 tbsp
- Lemon juice: 1 tsp

Exhibit 2-2: Recipe ingredients structured as an unordered list

Do it!

A-3: Creating an unordered list

Here's how — **Here's why**

1. Under the News archive heading, enter the following bold code:

   ```
   <h2>News archive</h2>
   <ul>
    <p>January - June 2012</p>
    <p>July - December 2011</p>
    <p>January - June 2011</p>
   </ul>
   ```

   Why: To start an unordered list.

2. Change each <p> tag to an <li> tag, as shown:

   ```
   <h2>News archive</h2>
   <ul>
    <li>January - June 2012</li>
    <li>July - December 2011</li>
    <li>January - June 2011</li>
   </ul>
   ```

3. Save your changes and reload the page in Firefox

   Why:

   News archive

   - January – June 2012
   - July – December 2011
   - January – June 2011

   The archive items appear as an unordered (bulleted) list.

4. Close the file in Notepad and Firefox

Ordered lists

Explanation

Use an *ordered list* to define items that follow a specific sequence or hierarchy. The <ol> tag defines an ordered list and contains individual list items defined by <li> tags. For example, the following code will produce the result shown in Exhibit 2-3.

```
<ol>
 <li>Heat olive oil in a large pan. </li>
 <li>Add the sliced onions and fry until transparent; then add
     ginger and garlic.</li>
 <li>Add chicken and fry slowly until browned.</li>
</ol>
```

1. Heat olive oil in a large pan.
2. Stir in the sliced onions, ginger, and garlic.
3. Add chicken and fry slowly until browned.

Exhibit 2-3: Recipe instructions structured as an ordered list

Do it!

A-4: Creating an ordered list

The files for this activity are in Student Data folder **Unit 2\Topic A**.

Here's how	Here's why
1 In Firefox, open recipes.html	The page contains some lists that you'll modify.
2 In Notepad, open recipes.html	
3 Under "Directions," add the following bold code:	(Scroll down, if necessary.) To define each line as an item in an ordered list.

```
<p>Directions:</p>
<ol>
 <li>Whisk the yogurt with the paste.</li>
 <li>Heat oil and add onions, ginger, and garlic paste.</li>
 <li>Add potatoes and fry until golden brown.</li>
 <li>Add yogurt and mix in salt.</li>
 <li>After 5 min, add 1 cup water and bring to a boil.</li>
 <li>Reduce heat and cook until the gravy is thick.</li>
</ol>
```

4 Save and reload the page	Directions: 1. Whisk the yogurt with the paste. 2. Heat oil and add onions, ginger and garlic paste. 3. Add potatoes and fry until golden brown. 4. Add yogurt and mix in salt. 5. After 5 min, add 1 cup of water and bring to a boil. 6. Reduce heat and cook until the gravy is thick. The list appears with six sequential steps.

Definition lists

Explanation

Definition lists are intended to display terms and their definitions. You create a definition list container by using the <dl> (definition list) element. The items in a definition list consist of two parts—a term and a definition. The term is defined by the <dt> (definition term) element, and its definition is applied with the <dd> (definition description) element.

By default, text in a <dd> element appears indented on the next line after the definition term. For example, the following code will produce the result shown in Exhibit 2-4.

```
<dl>
 <dt>Cinnamon</dt>
 <dd>Cinnamon comes from the bark of a small evergreen
     tree, which is dried and rolled into scroll-shaped
     quills, which are then ground into a powder.
 </dd>

 <dt>Nutmeg </dt>
 <dd>Nutmeg comes from an evergreen tree whose fruit, called
     the nutmeg apple, is dried and ground into a powder.
 </dd>
</dl>
```

Cinnamon

  Cinnamon comes from the bark of a small evergreen tree, which is dried and rolled into scroll-shaped quills, which are then ground into a powder.

Nutmeg

  Nutmeg comes from an evergreen tree whose fruit, called the nutmeg apple, is dried and ground into a powder.

Exhibit 2-4: Two terms and their descriptions

Nested lists

You can insert a list inside another list to display items as sub-categories. By nesting lists in this way, you can create a deeper hierarchy of information. To do so, start the sub-list inside the <li> element that you want to associate with the sub-list. For example, if you want to create an ordered list with an item that contains a separate unordered sub-list, start the unordered list inside the list item, as the following code and Exhibit 2-5 demonstrate.

```
<ol>
 <li>Stuffing ingredients:
  <ul>
   <li>Cooked potatoes: 4 oz. </li>
   <li>Cooked cauliflower: 2 oz.</li>
   <li>Outlander parsley: 2 tsp</li>
   <li>Outlander dill seed: 1 tsp</li>
   <li>Mayonnaise: 1 tbsp</li>
   <li>Lemon juice: 1 tsp</li>
  </ul>
 </li>
</ol>
```

1. Stuffing ingredients:
    - Cooked potatoes: 4 oz.
    - Cooked cauliflower: 2 oz.
    - Outlander parsley: 2 tsp
    - Outlander dill seed: 1 tsp
    - Mayonnaise: 1 tbsp
    - Lemon juice: 1 tsp

Exhibit 2-5: An unordered list nested inside an ordered list

In the code, notice that the list item that contains the sub-list is not closed until after the sub-list is closed. This is proper list nesting; it ensures that the entire sub-list is associated with a particular item in its parent list.

In Exhibit 2-5, notice that the nested list labels (bullets) are different from the standard solid-black labels. Browsers apply different default list labels to distinguish each level in a list hierarchy. You can nest any number of lists inside another list.

Do it!

A-5: Creating a nested list

Here's how	Here's why
1 Switch to Notepad	
2 Scroll to view the Ingredients list	
3 Select the closing list-item tag for the third item, as shown	<ul> <li>Potatoes, quartered: 3 cups </li> <li>Yogurt: 1 cup </li> <li>Roast and grind to a paste:</li> <li>Almonds: 3 tbsp </li>
Press DELETE	To remove the closing tag. You'll close the list-item tag at the end of the nested list.
Press ↵ ENTER	
4 Add the following bold code:	To create a sub-list inside the third list item.

```
<ul>
 <li>Almonds: 3 tbsp </li>
 <li>Outlander cinnamon: 1 tsp </li>
 <li>Outlander nutmeg: 1 tsp </li>
 <li>Outlander coriander: 1 tsp </li>
 <li>Outlander red chili powder: 1 tsp </li>
</ul>
</li>
 <li>Chopped onions 1 cup </li>
 <li>Ginger paste: 2 tsp </li>
 <li>Garlic paste: 2 tsp </li>
</ul>
```

Here's how	Here's why
5 Save your changes	

6 Reload the page in Firefox	• Potatoes, quartered: 3 cups
	• Yogurt: 1 cup
	• Roast and grind to a paste:
	  ○ Almonds: 3 tbsp
	  ○ Outlander cinnamon: 1 tsp
	  ○ Outlander nutmeg: 1 tsp
	  ○ Outlander coriander: 1 tsp
	  ○ Outlander red chili powder: 1 tsp
	• Chopped onions 1 cup
	• Ginger paste: 2 tsp
	• Garlic paste: 2 tsp
	
	The nested list is indented below the parent list item.

7 Create a sub-list for the first item in the archive list, as shown

Recipes archive

- 2012
  - Second half
  - First half
- 2011
- 2010

(In the Recipes archive section.) Start a new unordered list inside the first list-item tag.

8 In your own site project(s), what types of content might you structure in a list format?

9 Close all open files

Topic B: Phrase elements

Explanation

Now that you have learned about most of the structural elements of HTML, you will continue to learn how to mark up HTML documents by using a variety of semantically meaningful *phrase elements*, which are elements intended to mark up specific words or phrases in the document text.

Block elements and inline elements

Most HTML elements are either block elements or inline elements. *Block elements* create new lines and occupy the full width of their parent element. Structural elements like headings, paragraphs, sections, and footers are all examples of block elements. In this topic, you'll explore several of the most common *inline elements* (also called *phrase elements* or *text-level elements*), which do not create new lines and occupy only the amount of space their content requires. They are meant to logically define words or phrases within a parent block element.

The <b> element

Use the `<b>` element, which stands for bold, to highlight words or phrases without imparting emphasis or importance. For example, you might want to call out product names and their prices within a paragraph of text, as follows:

```
<p>Our specials this week are <b>Morning Blend</b> and
<b>Outback Blend</b>, only <b>$4.99</b> per pound.</p>
```

Browsers format text inside a `<b>` element as bold by default.

The <i> element

You can use the `<i>` element, which stands for italic, to distinguish such things as terms and idioms, a word or phrase in another language, or the title of a work of art or literature. For example:

```
<p><i>Of Mice and Men</i> is her favorite novel.</p>
```

By default, browsers format text inside an `<i>` element in italics.

The <em> element

By default, browsers display text in an `<em>` element in italics, but its purpose is not the same as the `<i>` element. Use the `<em>` element to denote emphasis for a word or phrase. This distinction is important because many screen readers will speak with emphasis when text is inside an `<em>` element.

Depending on the language in use, the location of the emphasis can change the meaning or implied meaning of a sentence. For example, in example 1, *whole bean* is stressed, implying that only holiday blends that are whole, not ground, are available in decaf. In example 2, *holiday blends* is stressed, implying that only the holiday blends (and not other whole-bean coffees) are available in decaf.

```
1. <p>Our <em>whole bean</em> holiday blends are available in
decaf.</p>

2. <p>Our whole bean <em>holiday blends</em> are available in
decaf.</p>
```

The <strong> element

Use the <strong> element to mark important text. By default, text in a <strong> element appears in bold in most browsers.

```
<p>If you want to attend the conference, please note that
<strong>registration ends on October 15, 2013.</strong></p>
```

The <mark> element

The <mark> element is new in HTML5. It's used to highlight content that is relevant in a particular context or used for temporary reference, such as keywords returned in a search. The <mark> tag should not be used to imply emphasis or importance.

Sometimes the <mark> element might not be part of the original document markup but rather might occur because of a user's actions in an application. For example, an application might process some kind of user input—say, a search within a site, using that site's own search engine—and then output <mark> tags to highlight the user's search terms in the search results.

By default, modern browsers use a yellow background to highlight text in a <mark> element. You can use a style sheet to set your own style for this and other HTML elements.

The <cite> element

Use the <cite> element to denote a citation or reference to another source. The <cite> element should contain only the title of a work or publication, not the author's name or other related information. For example:

```
<p>The following report from <cite>Investor's Monthly</cite>
suggests that the market will rebound this year.</p>
```

The <cite> element is especially useful in footnotes and bibliographies. By default, browsers apply italics to text in a <cite> element.

The <dfn> element

Use the <dfn> element to indicate a defining instance of a term when that term is defined once in a document and is then used elsewhere without being defined. The paragraph or section that is its closest parent element should also contain the term's definition. For example:

```
<p><dfn>Onomatopoeia</dfn> is a word that sounds like itself,
for example, "thud" or "hiss."</p>
```

By default, browsers italicize text in a <dfn> element.

Programming-related markup

The following elements are not as commonly used because they're meant to define fragments of code or, in the case of <kbd>, keyboard instructions for a user:

- <code> — Defines a fragment of code.
- <kbd> — Indicates that the text should be entered by the user (via a keyboard).
- <samp> — Defines sample output from a script or program.
- <var> — Indicates a programming variable.

Do it!

B-1: Applying phrase elements

The files for this activity are in Student Data folder **Unit 2\Topic B**.

Here's how	Here's why
1 In Firefox, open about-us.html	
2 In Notepad, open about-us.html	
3 Use the <b> element to make **Alan Garver** bold	**A note about our history** By **Alan Garver**, President Wrap only the name in the <b> element.
4 Define the text **Global Trader** as a citation	(In the second paragraph of the article.) Use the <cite> element.
5 Save your changes and reload the page in Firefox	"Alan Garver" is bold, and "Global Trader" is italic.
6 Switch to Notepad	
7 In the last paragraph, emphasize **5%**	Use the <em> element.
8 Define the last sentence in the last paragraph as important	(Use the <strong> element.) Be sure the closing tag is properly nested in the paragraph.
9 Highlight **Outlander Club**	Use the <mark> element.
10 Save your changes and reload the page in Firefox	The last sentence is bold, "5%" is italic, and "Outlander Club" is highlighted in yellow, which is the default style that browsers apply to the <mark> element.
11 Describe a scenario in which an application could make specific use of the <dfn> element.	

Character entities

Explanation

When you need to display special characters like the copyright symbol (©) or registered symbol (®), you use *character entities.* These are not HTML elements per se, but special codes that represent symbols not available on standard keyboards. There are hundreds of character entities, but typically only a handful of them are needed for most English-language Web sites.

The following table lists some of the most common symbols and corresponding character entity codes.

Symbol	Entity	Description
®	®	Registered symbol
™	™	Trademark symbol
©	©	Copyright symbol
(none)		A nonbreaking space creates an empty space about the size of a single letter and does not create a line break.
¼	¼	The fraction one-quarter
½	½	The fraction one-half
¾	¾	The fraction three-quarters

The ampersand (`&`) indicates the beginning of a character entity, and the semi-colon (`;`) indicates its end. Case is important in these codes. Write them in lowercase, or browsers will display some codes as text, rather than displaying the desired symbol.

Do it!

B-2: Applying character entities

Here's how	Here's why
1 Switch to Notepad	You'll continue to modify the about-us.html page.

2 In the footer section, select **copyright**	`<footer>`
	`<p>Contents copyright 2010-2015`
	`</footer>`

3 Type **©**	To replace the text "copyright" with the character entity for the copyright symbol.
4 Save your changes and reload the page in Firefox	
5 Switch to Notepad	
6 Remove the `<mark>` tags around "Outlander Club"	Select the opening tag and press Delete; then select the closing tag and press Delete. Or press the Backspace key to clear the tags.
7 Place the insertion point where shown	`Outlander Club.` (Click between "Club" and the period.) You'll insert the Trademark symbol here.
8 Type **™**	To insert the character entity for the Trademark symbol.
9 Save your changes and reload the page in Firefox	the Outlander Club™. The Trademark symbol is displayed.
10 Close all open files	

Topic C: Attributes

Explanation

Now that you have learned about several HTML elements, you will continue to create pages by incorporating attributes, which allow you to specify information about elements and augment your document structure.

Attribute syntax

Attributes provide information about elements. They are specified within the tag, after the tag name. In the following example, the `lang` attribute of the `<html>` element specifies that the document's primary language is English.

```
<html lang="en">
```

Attributes are optional and are allowed only in opening tags. Many attributes are exclusive to certain elements, while other attributes are global and can be used in a variety of elements.

Global attributes

The global attributes are those attributes that can be applied to any HTML element. There are several global attributes, and some of them become relevant only in more advanced contexts. Some of the most commonly used global attributes are `lang`, `class`, and `id`.

The lang attribute

You can use the `lang` attribute to specify the primary language of a page or the language of a specific element in a page. Specifying the language of a page or section can help search engines determine relevance, and it can help alternative devices like screen readers identify changes in the natural language.

For example, if you have a document whose primary language is English, and you use a French term within a paragraph, you would write:

```
<p>Thanks for your order. <i lang="fr">Bon appétit!</i></p>
```

The `<i>` element is chosen to create italics without implying stress emphasis. In this example, the change in the document language is limited to the scope of the `<i>` element because the attribute is in that tag. The document then reverts to `lang="en"` as soon as the `<i>` element is closed.

Some of the most common language codes are `en` for English, `es` for Spanish, `de` for German, and `fr` for French.

The id attribute

The id attribute is a global attribute that serves as a unique identifier for an element on a page. It's typically used to uniquely identify major page sections. For example:

```
<section id="mainContent">
 Other elements and content...
</section>
```

It's important to use meaningful ID names. The purpose is to create elements and sections that describe the content they contain or the role they play in the overall structure or design. Choose an ID that will be meaningful to other developers who need to read and modify the code. For example, ID names like "mainContent" and "orderForm" are more meaningful and effective than "areaB" or "coolSection."

Each ID must be unique to a page. For example, the "mainContent" ID in the previous example should not appear more than once per document.

Other advantages of using the id attribute include:

- You can attach CSS styles to IDs.
- You can link directly to an element with an ID.
- Applications and scripts can interact with element IDs.

The class attribute

The class attribute is a global attribute that you can use to classify elements. For example, you might want to create a special class of the <p> element named "credit" to contain the names of content authors. The "credit" classification semantically distinguishes a paragraph from other paragraphs. Unlike the id attribute, classes are not unique to a page; a class name can be shared among multiple elements in a document.

Your class names can be anything you want, but again, it's important to choose a name that describes the role that an element plays in the structure or design or provides some level of description for the content. For example:

```
<p><strong class="warning">Do not click the Back button while
your order is processing.</strong></p>
```

Applying meaningful class names is another way you can enhance and extend document structure beyond the predefined structural elements of HTML.

Do it!

C-1: Applying attributes

The files for this activity are in Student Data folder **Unit 2\Topic C**.

Here's how	Here's why
1 In Firefox, open latest-news.html	You'll add attributes to some of the page's elements.
2 In Notepad, open latest-news.html	
3 Add the following bold code to the `<html>` tag: `<html` **`lang="en"`**`>`	To define the document's primary language as English. Setting this attribute can help search engines determine relevance, and help devices like screen readers identify changes in the natural language.
4 Add the following bold code to the `<nav>` element: `<nav` **`id="siteNav"`**`>`	To define the content of this element as the site's primary navigation.
5 Can the "siteNav" ID be used elsewhere in this document?	
6 Locate the first `<section>` element	The section contains the "Company news" header and one paragraph. You'll modify this section structure.
7 Add the following bold code to the first `<section>` element: `<section` **`id="news">`**	
8 Close this section after the "News archive" closing section tag	(Directly above the page footer.) This section now contains all the news items.
9 Locate the first paragraph	Scroll up, if necessary.
Observe the extra closing section tag after the paragraph	This tag originally closed the "news" section. Now it will be the closing tag for a new section.
10 Create a new `<section>` element, as shown:	To create a new section inside the outer news section.

```
<section>
<p>
Outlander Spices is now ISO 9000 certified, reflecting our
commitment to providing only the finest quality products.
</p>

</section>
```

(In the code above, the opening `<section>` tag is printed in bold.)

11 Give the new section the following ID:

```
<section id="latestNews">
<p>
Outlander Spices is now ISO 9000 certified, reflecting our
commitment to providing only the finest quality products.
</p>

</section>
```

12 Add the following heading:

```
<section id="latestNews">
<h3>ISO certification</h3>
<p>
Outlander Spices is now ISO 9000 certified, reflecting our
commitment to providing only the finest quality products.
</p>

</section>
```

Each section should have a heading. If a heading does not seem appropriate for the content, then that material probably shouldn't be defined as a section.

13 In the article, add the following bold code:

```
<p class="credit">By <b>Alan Garver</b>, President</p>
```

14 Can the "credit" class be used elsewhere in this document?

15 Save your changes

Quotations

Explanation

When your document contains quotations, you should define them as such. Use the `<blockquote>` element to define long quotes, and use the `<q>` element to define short, inline quotes. Both elements use the `cite` attribute to indicate the source of the quote.

Block quotations

As its name suggests, the `<blockquote>` element is a block element, so it creates a line break. Browsers also indent text in a `<blockquote>` element on both sides. Use this element with the `cite` attribute to provide the source of the quote. For example:

```
<blockquote cite="http://en.wikipedia.org/wiki/HTML5">
"HTML5 is a language for structuring and presenting content
for the World Wide Web, a core technology of the Internet."
</blockquote>
```

Sometimes the `cite` attribute isn't necessary—for example, if the source of the quote is obvious in its context or has already been referenced or credited. Often, however, a quotation without a reference to its source is unhelpful, and in some cases can even violate copyright laws. Putting this level of care and quality into your markup will make your documents more interoperable, searchable, professional, and usable.

Inline quotations

You can use the `<q>` element to define short, inline quotations, using the `cite` attribute to provide a valid URL for the source. For example:

```
<p>HTML5 <q cite="http://en.wikipedia.org/wiki/HTML5">extends,
improves and rationalizes the markup available for
documents</q> on the Web. </p>
```

Browsers automatically insert quotation marks around text inside a `<q>` element, so it's important to omit them in the code, or there will be duplicate quotation marks. If you prefer not to mark up inline quotations and to rely on devices to insert quotation marks, it's also valid to simply use quotation marks and omit the `<q>` element. However, you should still cite the source of the quote, either in the text or as a footnote.

Abbreviations and acronyms

Use the `<abbr>` element to define abbreviations and acronyms. Use the `title` attribute to provide the full version of the abbreviated word. For example:

```
<p><abbr title="National Aeronautics and Space
Administration">NASA</abbr> engineers cheered when they
received a response from their Mars rover, named Spirit.</p>
```

It's important to include the `title` attribute whenever you define an abbreviation or acronym, because in most browsers, users can display the full version of the phrase by pointing to it. A ScreenTip appears, showing the content of the `title` attribute.

In addition, Firefox automatically applies a dotted underline to text in an <abbr> tag that also contains a title attribute, as shown in Exhibit 2-6. This visual cue tells the user that more information is available. You can use a style sheet to customize this style and make it look the same in all browsers.

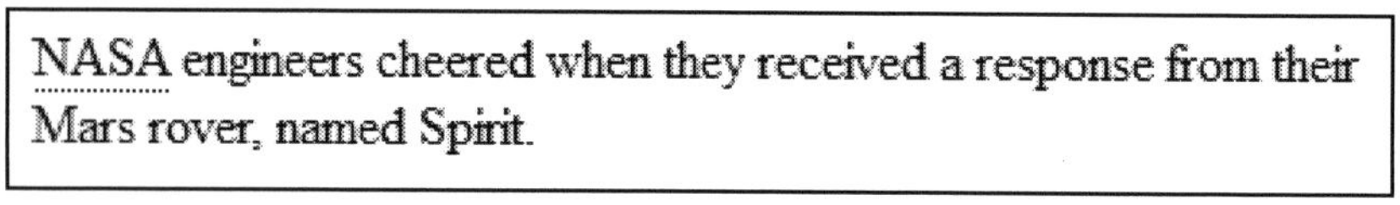

NASA engineers cheered when they received a response from their Mars rover, named Spirit.

Exhibit 2-6: The default style applied to abbreviations in Firefox.

Do it!

C-2: Defining quotes and abbreviations

Here's how	Here's why
1 In the second paragraph, click directly before "U.S."	To place the insertion point there.
2 Type the following:	To define an inline quotation and its source.
`<q cite="http://outlanderspices.com/GT-article.html">`	
3 After "1966," close the inline quote	Click after the end of the sentence and add a closing </q> tag.
4 Change the third paragraph to a block quote	(The paragraph that begins with "As always….") Change the opening and closing paragraph tags to blockquote tags.
5 In the first section paragraph, add the following bold code:	(Scroll up.) To define ISO as an abbreviation.
`<p>Outlander Spices is now` **`<abbr>`**`ISO`**`</abbr>`** `9000 certified, reflecting our commitment to providing only the finest quality products.</p>`	
6 Add the following bold code:	
`<abbr` **`title="International Organization for Standardization">`**`ISO</abbr>`	
7 Save your changes and reload the page in Firefox	
8 Observe the abbreviation	By default, Firefox applies a dotted underline style to abbreviations that have a `title` attribute. This style indicates that more information is available.
Point to the abbreviation	A ScreenTip appears, showing the content of the `title` attribute.
9 Locate the inline quote	Notice that quotation marks appear even though they are not part of the document content. Browsers automatically apply quotation marks to text inside the <q> element.
10 Observe the default formatting applied to the block quote	By default, browsers indent text in a <blockquote> element.
11 Close all open files	

Unit summary: Elements and attributes

Topic A

In this topic, you learned how to define a **document structure** by using semantically meaningful elements, including <header>, <section>, <nav>, and <footer>. You learned about the **advantages** of creating a meaningful document structure, and you learned how to create three kinds of **lists**: ordered lists, unordered lists, and nested lists.

Topic B

In this topic, you learned that **phrase elements** mark up specific words or phrases in the document text. You learned about the difference between **block elements** and **inline elements**, and you applied several phrase elements, including <em>, <strong>, <mark>. and <cite>. You also learned how to add **character entities** to display characters that are not available on standard keyboards.

Topic C

In this topic, you learned that **attributes** provide information about elements. You learned that global attributes can apply to all elements, and there are other attributes that are unique to various elements. You applied the **lang**, **id**, and **class** attributes, and you used the **cite** attribute inside the <blockquote> and <q> elements to define quotations and their sources.

Independent practice activity

In this activity, you will create a page structure with several elements, and apply phrase elements and attributes to mark up text.

The files for this activity are in Student Data folder **Unit 2\Unit summary**.

1 In Firefox, open gdb-aboutus.html.

2 In Notepad, open gdb-aboutus.html.

3 Specify that this document is in the English language. (*Hint:* The language code for English is `en`.)

4 Change the first paragraph to a `<nav>` element with the ID **siteNav**.

5 Define the top two headings as a header group.

6 Define the copyright paragraph at the bottom as a footer.

7 Change the word "copyright" to the character entity for the copyright symbol.

8 Change the short series of paragraphs beginning with "First editions" and ending with "Arts & sciences" into an unordered list, with each paragraph being a list item. (*Hint:* Change each pair of opening and closing `<p>` tags into opening and closing `<li>` tags.)

9 Put the last paragraph (the one that begins with "We carry…") in its own `<section>` element with the ID **offer**.

10 Starting after the header group, put the rest of the content, all the way to the end of the unordered list, in a `<section>` element with the ID **main**.

11 Define text "Register before August 1st" as important text, and give it the class name **deadline**.

12 Save your changes, and reload the page in Firefox to verify your results.

13 Close all open windows.

Review questions

1 True or false? A search engine will likely produce better results if a page is well structured and the content is marked up meaningfully.

2 What is meant by "semantically meaningful" elements?

3 True or false? The <hgroup> element should contain only a group of heading tags (h1 through h6).

4 Which elements are not allowed inside a <header> element? [Choose all that apply.]

A <header>

B <p>

C <h6>

D <footer>

5 True or false? A <section> element can contain other <section> elements.

6 What is a benefit of the independent header structures that can be used within each <section> element?

7 True or false? Each section should have a heading.

8 In a definition list, each item consists of which two parts?

A A <dl> element and a definition (the <dd> element)

B A definition term (<dt>) and a definition description (<dd>)

C A definition and a reference to a source

D A <dl> element and a definition term (<dt>)

9 What is a key difference between an ID and a class?

10 What's the difference between a block element and an inline element?

11 Which of the following are block elements? [Choose all that apply.]

A <h1>

B <section>

C <nav>

D <cite>

12 Which of the following are phrase (inline) elements? [Choose all that apply.]

A <em>

B <footer>

C <mark>

D <strong>

Unit 3
Style sheets

Unit time: 150 minutes

Complete this unit, and you'll know how to:

A Write CSS styles, embed a style sheet, apply color, and create an external style sheet and link pages to it.

B Control font and font size, text alignment, line height, and letter spacing.

C Control box styles, including borders, padding, margins, height, and width, and create rounded corners and shadows.

Topic A: Introduction to style sheets

Explanation

HTML elements and attributes are used to structure and define content, but not format it. For that, you need to use a style sheet.

Formatting content with CSS

CSS stands for *Cascading Style Sheets*. It's the standard style language of the Web. A *style sheet* is a text file that contains rules that specify how various HTML elements are displayed on a Web page. Along with HTML, JavaScript, and other technologies, CSS helps to make the Web a platform for rich, interactive sites and applications.

Style sheet syntax

Style rules have a syntax that's easy to learn and use. You select the HTML element that you want to apply a style to, and then specify the style or series of styles you want to apply, in the following format:

```
selector { property: value; property: value; }
```

Each style sheet rule begins with a *selector*, which specifies the HTML element to be formatted. This can be any valid HTML element—just remove the brackets from the tag name and you have a selector. For example, your selector might be `blockquote`, `h1`, `section`, `footer`, or `p`.

After the selector comes one or more *properties* and their corresponding values, which define the formatting applied to the selected element. Properties and values are separated by a colon, and property-value pairs are terminated with a semicolon. All the properties and values in a rule are enclosed in a single set of braces. For example, to make the text of all paragraphs navy blue, you'd write the following style rule:

```
p { color: navy; }
```

In this example, `p` is the selector, `color` is the property, and `navy` is the value.

Embedded style sheets

You can embed a style sheet in an HTML document to control the presentation of that single page, or you can link multiple documents to an external style sheet to control the presentation of multiple pages from a single source.

To create an embedded style sheet, you insert a `<style>` container inside the `<head>` section of your HTML page, and then insert your style rules inside the `<style>` container, as follows:

```
<!DOCTYPE html>
<html lang="en">
<head>
<title>My Document</title>
<style>
p { color: navy; }
h1 { font-size: 24px; }
</style>
</head>

<body>
...all your HTML content...
</body>
</html>
```

Prior to HTML5, the `<style>` element required a `type="text/css"` attribute and value. However, modern browsers assume this as the default style type, so you don't have to write it explicitly.

Do it!

A-1: Embedding a style sheet

The files for this activity are in Student Data folder **Unit 3\Topic A**.

Here's how	Here's why
1 In Firefox, open update.html	This page already has a structure set up. You'll begin to apply styles to page elements.
2 In Notepad, open update.html	
3 In the head container, type the following bold code:	To create an empty style container.

```
<head>
<title>Outlander Coffees & Spices: News</title>
<style>

</style>
</head>
```

In the style container, you will create style rules specific to this page.

Here's how	Here's why
4 Save your changes and reload the page in Firefox	There is no change because there are no style rules yet in the style container.
5 Switch to Notepad and add the following bold code:	(In the style container.) To make all paragraphs be displayed with navy blue text.

```
<style>

p { color: navy; }

</style>
```

Here's how	Here's why
Save your changes	
6 Reload the page in Firefox and scroll to observe all the text	Only text inside a <p> element is navy blue.
7 Switch to Notepad and change the selector from "p" to **h2**	To make only level-two headings navy blue.
Verify the result in Firefox	(Reload the page.) The paragraphs return to the default color, black, and the <h2> headings are navy blue.

Hexadecimal color values

Explanation

There are several predefined color-name keywords that you can use to apply color values, such as navy, orange, silver, or violet, but there are far more permutations of color available through the use of hexadecimal codes.

Hexadecimal color values are codes that represent different RGB combinations. *RGB* is short for red, green, and blue. Hexadecimal codes all begin with a pound sign (#), followed by three pairs of numbers or letters in the range 0 through 9 and A through F, respectively. The first two alphanumeric pair denotes the intensity of red in the color, the second pair denotes the intensity of green, and the third, blue.

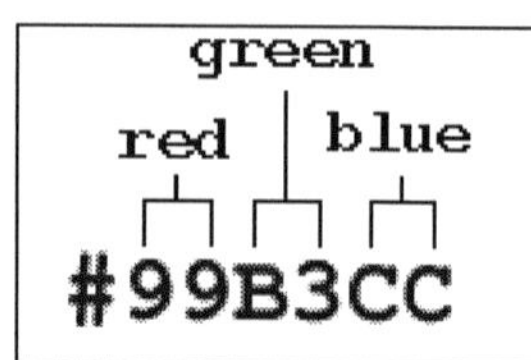

Exhibit 3-1: A hexadecimal color code (for a grayish blue)

For example, the hexadecimal code #000000 is black—zero value for red, blue, and green. Conversely, #FFFFFF is white—full intensity of red, blue, and green. Hexadecimal codes are not case sensitive, so you can write them in upper- or lowercase text, as you prefer.

With a few exceptions, hexadecimal color codes aren't easy to remember, but there's no point in trying to. There are countless hexadecimal color charts on the Web that you can use for reference. In addition, most full-featured HTML editing applications include color swatches so that you can select colors without having to manually write hexadecimal values. There are more than 16 million hexadecimal color values.

Shorthand values

When a hexadecimal color value has matching R,G, and B values, such as #33BBFF, or #99AA99, you can reduce each pair to a single value, as in #3BF and #9A9.

Do it!

A-2: Applying color with hexadecimal values

Here's how	Here's why
1 Switch to Notepad	
2 Change "navy" to **#006633**	(In the style rule.) To make the level-two headings green.
3 Save your changes and reload the page in Firefox	The level-two headings change from blue to green.

4 Add the following bold code:
`<style>`
 	
`h2 { color: #006633; }`
`footer { color: #063; }`
 	
`</style>`
	To give the footer text the same green color by using a shorthand value.

Save your changes and reload the page in Firefox	The footer text now has the same green color.
5 Change the color value for the h2 rule to its shorthand equivalent	
6 Save your change and reload the page in Firefox	There should be no change in the green heading color.

Background color

Explanation

You can set an element's background color by using the `background-color` property. For example, to give all level-one headings a gray background, you could write:

```
h1 { background-color: gray; }
```

When you apply a background color to a block element, the color fills the entire width of the element's containing area, which is defined by its parent element. If the parent element is the `<body>` element, the width of the element is determined by the size of the user's browser window, unless a width value is explicitly set. For example, Exhibit 3-2 shows a heading and a paragraph, each with a background color that fills the entire available width for each element.

This is a heading

This is a paragraph. Like the heading, the background color fills the entire width of the available space.

Exhibit 3-2: Background colors applied to block elements

When you apply a background color to an inline element, the color extends only to the width of the element text, as shown in Exhibit 3-3.

This month only: take an additional $10 off the following out-of-print titles:

Exhibit 3-3: Background color applied to an inline element

Color contrast

When you apply background color, it's important that you choose a color that provides sufficient contrast with the element's text color. When the text color and background color do not have sufficient contrast, the result can strain the eyes and make the text difficult to read.

Grouping properties

You can group properties in a style rule. This feature allows you to apply multiple styles to an element without having to write a whole new rule for each style. To group properties, separate each property and its value with a semicolon. For example, to give level-one headings navy blue text and a silver background, you would write:

```
h1 { color: navy; background-color: silver; }
```

Grouping selectors

If you want a style to apply to more than one element, you can group selectors into a single rule by separating them with commas. For example, if you want all level-one headings and paragraphs to have a silver background color, you could write:

```
h1, p { background-color: silver; }
```

This is a more efficient way of writing:

```
h1 { background-color: silver; }
p { background-color: silver; }
```

By combining the two selectors, you can save time, reduce error and redundancies, and keep your style sheet code as lean as possible.

Do it!

A-3: Setting background colors

Here's how	Here's why
1 Delete the footer rule	
2 Add the following to the h2 selector:	To consolidate the two rules into one.
`h2, footer { color: #063; }`	
3 Add the following bold code to the rule:	To apply a light gray background color to both the h2 and footer elements.
`h2, footer { color: #063; background-color: #eee; }`	
4 Save your changes and view the result in Firefox	(Scroll down to see the footer, if necessary.) The headings and footer now have green text and a light gray background.
Switch to Notepad	
5 Add the following style rule:	
`nav { background-color: #f87217; }`	To give the link section a dark orange background color.
Save your changes and view the result in Firefox	The `<nav>` section now has an orange background.
6 Can the background color value in the previous step be reduced to a shorthand equivalent? Why or why not?	

External style sheets

Explanation

With an external style sheet, you can control the design and layout of all your site pages. No matter how many pages a site consists of, it can be updated by modifying a single style sheet file. An external style sheet is a text file that contains only CSS style rules. It cannot contain any HTML elements, and it must be saved with a .css extension, as in mystyles.css. Most Web sites use external style sheets to store global (shared) styles, which establish a consistent look and feel across all site pages.

Another key advantage of using external style sheets is the separation of content and style information. When you keep all formatting instructions separate from your content, your pages can remain lean, efficient, and easy to modify.

You should create separate folders to store each type of site asset, such as style sheets, images, scripts, and videos. This approach helps keep your site's directory structure tidy and easy to maintain.

Do it!

A-4: Creating an external style sheet

The files for this activity are in Student Data folder **Unit 3\Topic A**.

Here's how	Here's why
1 Using Windows Explorer, open the styles folder	(In the current topic folder.) The folder is empty. Site resources such as style sheets, scripts, and images should be stored in separate folders.
Right-click in the empty window	To open the shortcut menu.
Choose **New**, **Text Document**	To create a text file in Notepad. The file name is selected for editing.
2 Drag to select the default file name and the file extension	You'll rename the file and give it a new file extension.
Type **styles.css**	To name the file with the proper file extension for a style sheet.
Press ENTER	A dialog box opens.
Press ENTER	(Or click Yes.) To close the dialog box and rename the file.
3 Double-click **styles.css**	To open the file. (If a dialog box appears, verify that Notepad is selected, select Always use the selected program to open this kind of file, and click OK.)
4 Switch to update.html	(The Notepad file.) You'll cut the rules from the embedded style sheet and put them in the external style sheet.
5 Select the style rules	Select only the rules, and not the `<style>` container.
Press CTRL + X	To cut the rules from the style sheet.
6 Switch to styles.css	
Press CTRL + V	To paste the rules into the external style sheet.
Press CTRL + S	To save the style sheet.

The <link> element

Explanation

With the `<link>` element, you can link your pages to other resources, such as style sheets and scripts. The `<link>` element is used inside a document's head section and has two required attributes, `href` and `rel`.

The `href` attribute specifies the hypertext reference (the location and file name) of the style sheet or other resource. In the example that follows, the style sheet mystyles.css is located in a folder named stylesheets.

The `rel` attribute specifies the relationship of the referenced file to the main document. In this example, the `rel` attribute indicates that the referenced file is a style sheet.

```
<link rel="stylesheet" href="stylesheets/mystyles.css" />
```

Also, notice that the element is terminated with a slash at the end of the tag. The `<link>` element is an *empty element*, meaning that it's not a container and therefore does not have a corresponding closing tag. HTML5 does not require a terminating slash for empty elements, but you can include one if you prefer to follow the authoring standards of XHTML, which requires that all tags be closed.

Multiple style sheet sources

A page can contain multiple `<link>` elements, linking the page to several style sheets. You might want to create separate style sheets for mobile devices or for optimizing the print output of your pages. A page that's linked to one or more external style sheets can also contain its own embedded style sheet. The external style sheet would control all styles shared by multiples pages ("global" styles), while the embedded style sheet would contain styles that apply only to that page.

Do it!

A-5: Linking pages to a style sheet

The files for this activity are in Student Data folder **Unit 3\Topic A**.

Here's how	Here's why
1 Switch to update.html	In Notepad.
Click before the opening `<style>` container	To place the insertion point.
Press ENTER twice	
2 In the space above the `<style>` tag, type the following code:	
`<link rel="stylesheet" href="styles/styles.css" />`	
3 Save your changes	
4 Switch to Firefox and reload update.html	There should be no visible change; the styles were moved from the internal (embedded) style sheet to the external style sheet to control the formatting of multiple pages.
5 In Firefox, open recipes.html	(From the current topic folder.) This page contains many of the same structures as the update.html page. You'll link this page to the external style sheet.
6 Switch to update.html and copy the entire `<link>` element	Select it and then press Ctrl+C or choose Edit, Copy.
7 In Notepad, open recipes.html	From the current topic folder.
Paste the `<link>` element inside the head section	
Save your changes	Press Ctrl+S or choose File, Save.
8 Reload recipes.html in Firefox	The page picks up the same styles as the update.html page. Using an external style sheet allows you to make global changes by editing a single source and to maintain a consistent look and feel throughout your site.

The cascade

Explanation

The *cascading* part of Cascading Style Sheets refers to the way styles are resolved when conflicts arise. A conflict happens when two or more style rules try to influence an element with the same property. For example, say you have a page that's linked to an external style sheet and that also has an embedded style sheet. If a rule in the external style sheet gives all paragraphs navy blue text, while a rule in the page's embedded style sheet gives all paragraphs black text, which style rule wins out?

The more specific or local a style, the more importance it has. In the previous example, the page with an embedded style sheet that gives all paragraphs black text will override the rule (for navy blue text) in the external style sheet because the embedded style sheet is closer, or more local to, the HTML element that's being styled.

If the rule in the external style sheet gives all paragraphs an additional style that is not specified in the embedded style sheet, that style will be applied because there is no conflict between style sheets.

When to put styles in an external style sheet

Whenever you want a style to be global (shared among multiple documents), put that style in an external style sheet. This way, there's no duplication of code and you can update multiple pages from one source.

When to put styles in an embedded style sheet

When deciding where to place a particular style rule, think about how to create optimal efficiency. For example, if you have a style that is used by only one page, embed the style in that document by using a `<style>` container. Otherwise, if you were to place a style that's specific to one page in an external style sheet, all the other pages in the site would needlessly access that style rule.

Do it!

A-6: Exploring cascading styles

Here's how	Here's why
1 In Firefox, switch to update.html	Click the other page tab.
Observe the "Company news" heading	The external style sheet contains a rule that makes this heading green.
2 Switch to the update.html file	In Notepad.
3 In the `<style>` container, enter the following rule: `h2 { color: #f60; }`	
4 Save your changes and reload the page in Firefox	The heading is orange because the embedded style is more local than the conflicting rule in the external style sheet, which applies a green text color.
5 Change the rule as follows: `h2 { background-color: #fc6; }`	
6 Save your changes and reload the page in Firefox	The background color is now a light orange because this rule is closer than the conflicting style in the external style sheet that makes it gray. The text color reverts to green because the embedded rule does not include a style that conflicts with it. The heading is styled by rules in both the embedded style sheet and the external style sheet.
7 Close all open files	
8 If you want all block quotes in your site to have a gray background color, should you put the style rule in an external or embedded style sheet?	
9 If you want block quotes in one particular page of your site to have a light green background color, should you put the style rule in an external or embedded style sheet?	

Topic B: Basic text and font styles

Explanation

By default, browsers display text in a font called Times New Roman. If this font doesn't suit your design, you can change it with CSS. You can also change the font size of any text element to improve the readability of your content and make your Web pages look more distinguished.

Setting the font

To change the font of a text element, you use the `font-family` property in a style sheet. For example, to set the font for all text, you can use `body` as your selector, as follows:

```
body { font-family: Verdana; }
```

To ensure that your site visitors will view your text in the intended font or a similar font, you should always specify at least two or three fonts, with each one separated by a comma, as follows:

```
body { font-family: Verdana, Geneva, Arial, sans-serif; }
```

This way, a user's browser will try to load the first font in the list. If the user does not have that font installed, the browser will try the second, then the third, and so on until a match is made. If the font you choose consists of multiple words, you need to enclose them in quotes, as follows:

```
body { font-family: "Trebuchet MS", Georgia, serif; }
```

Generic families: serif and sans serif

You should end your font family list with either *serif* or *sans serif*, as shown above. These designations are called *generic families*, and they ensure that all users, no matter what operating system and platform their computers are running on, will be able to read your text in a font that is similar to your first choice.

A serif font is one that has *flourishes*, small embellishments at the tips of its letters, like the text you're reading now. A sans-serif font is one that does not have any flourishes at the tips of its letters, as shown in Exhibit 3-4.

This is text in a sans serif font.

Exhibit 3-4: Sans serif text

Common serif fonts include Times New Roman, Times, Georgia, and Garamond. Common sans serif fonts include Verdana, Arial, Geneva, and Helvetica. No matter what font you choose as your site's primary font, you should use it consistently on all of your site's pages. Avoid using too many different fonts; doing so can make a Web site look cluttered and amateurish.

Inheritance

Inheritance is another aspect of the cascade (how styles are resolved when conflicts arise). For most text and font styles, inheritance can be passed from parent elements to child elements. This means that, for example, if you set a font for the `<body>` element, all elements on the page will share that font because the `<body>` element is the top-level parent element. Similarly, if you set the font for only paragraphs, any elements within a `<p>` element will inherit the same font.

If you don't want an element to inherit a style, simply create a style for that element. For example, if you give the `<body>` element the font Geneva to establish the default font, but you want all headings to be displayed in the font Arial, create a rule that applies that font to the headings.

Do it!

B-1: Setting the font

The files for this activity are in Student Data folder **Unit 3\Topic B**.

Here's how	Here's why
1 In Firefox, open about.html	This page is already linked to an external style sheet named globalstyles.css.
2 In Notepad, open globalstyles.css	From the styles folder, in the current topic folder.
3 Add the following new rule to the style sheet:	To establish a new default font.
`body { font-family: Verdana, Geneva, sans-serif; }`	
	All text elements are child elements of the `<body>` element, so they will all inherit this style.
4 Save the style sheet and reload the page in Firefox	All text on the page is now displayed with the font Verdana, a sans serif font that's installed on Windows-based computers. The text looks larger because characters in Verdana are larger than characters in Times New Roman at the same font size.
5 Switch to the style sheet	
Add the following rule:	To set a different font for the headings.
`h1,h2,h3 { font-family: Georgia, Garamond, serif; }`	
6 Save your changes and reload the page in Firefox	The headings now appear in the font Georgia, a serif font that's installed on Windows-based computers. The other content continues to inherit the font from the body rule.

Font size

Explanation

To set the font size for a text element, you use the `font-size` property, followed by a value. Browsers use 16 pixels as the default font size. (Computer screens are measured in terms of pixels.) To set font size, you need to first indicate the number of pixels, and then add `px`, with no space in between, as follows:

```
body { font-size: 14px; }
```

In an external style sheet, this rule will create a new default font size for all text elements. Some fonts will appear bigger than others at the same font size. For example, an Arial font at 16px appears bigger than Times New Roman at 16px. This difference occurs because the alphanumeric characters that make up different fonts are all slightly different in size—it has nothing to do with the font size values you apply.

Absolute and relative units of measurement

Pixel values are an effective unit of measurement when you're using the `font-size` property because pixels are a unit of screen measurement, as opposed to units of print measurement, like points and picas. Using pixels produces consistent results in several browsers and platforms.

Using pixels as a unit of measurement creates what's called an *absolute value*, meaning that the text will be displayed at the size specified. You can also use a *relative value*, which is a percentage value calculated relative to a parent element. For example, if the font size for the body element is 20px and you set the font size for footer elements to 50%, text in a footer element will be displayed at 10px, or one-half of its parent's font size.

Another relative unit of measurement is the em unit. In terms of font size, 1em is equivalent to 100%, so a value of 2em is the same as 200%, and 0.5em is equivalent to 50%.

Do it!

B-2: Controlling font size

Here's how	Here's why
1 Switch to the style sheet	

Add the following bold code to the body rule:
`body { font-family: Verdana, Geneva, sans-serif;`
`       **font-size: 14px;** }`	

2 Save your changes and reload the page in Firefox	The text looks smaller than before because the default font size is 16px. Notice that the headings retain their font size hierarchy, with the top-level heading being the largest. Headings inherit font sizes differently depending on the browser. To control the font size of headings and ensure consistent results, you must style them specifically.

3 Add the following rules:
`h1 { font-size: 24px; }`
`h2 { font-size: 18px; }`
`h3 { font-size: 16px; }`
	To set the font size for the headings.

4 Save your changes and reload the page in Firefox	The headings are smaller than before but are still proportional to each other to visually indicate the heading hierarchy.
5 Add the following rule: `blockquote { font-size: 130%; }`	
Save your changes and reload the page in Firefox	The block quote text is now displayed at 130% of the inherited font size.
6 Add the following rule: `footer { font-size: 70%; }`	
7 Save your changes and reload the page in Firefox	
View the footer text	(Scroll down, if necessary.) The footer text appears at 70% of the inherited font size.

Line height, letter spacing, and text alignment

Explanation

You can use CSS to control several aspects of text formatting. For example, you can control the spacing between adjacent lines of text, the space between individual letters, and the alignment of text on a page.

Line height

Line height refers to the height of the lines of text in an element. You control line height by using the `line-height` property. You can apply an absolute height value such as 8px, a relative value such as 120%, or a positive integer value, such as 2 or 1.6. (Negative values are not allowed.) Both percentage values and integer values are multiplied by the element's font size to determine the element's line height. For example, a value of 2 creates a line height value equal to two times the element's font size, which is the same as specifying a value of 200%.

By default, browsers apply a line height equivalent to approximately 1.25 times the font size. Line spacing is also referred to as *leading* (pronounced "ledding").

Letter spacing

You can use the `letter-spacing` property to increase or decrease the amount of space between adjacent characters in a text element. You specify letter spacing by using values such as 4px or .5em. Negative values such as -2px are allowed if you want to reduce the amount of default spacing between characters. Letter spacing is also called *tracking.*

Text alignment

You can align text by using the `text-align` property. You can specify the `left`, `right`, `center`, or `justify` value. When you use the `justify` value, the spacing between words is adjusted so that each line of text in the element is of equal length. Justification often results in varying degrees of word spacing on each line, and this might not be the desired result. It's important that your text styles don't detract from the readability of your content. It can be helpful to involve several people to help you determine which combination of styles results in optimal clarity and readability.

Do it!

B-3: Controlling line height, letter spacing, and alignment

Here's how	Here's why
1 Add the following rule: `p { line-height: 1.5; }`	To increase the line height between adjacent lines of text in paragraphs.
2 Save your changes and reload the page in Firefox	The paragraph line spacing has increased.
3 Add the following bold code to the p rule: `p { line-height: 1.5;` **`text-align: justify;`** `}`	To justify text in paragraphs.
4 Save your changes and reload the page in Firefox	The spacing of text in the paragraphs is adjusted so that all lines are the same length.
5 Add the following bold code to the footer rule: `footer { font-size: 70%;` **`text-align: center;`** `}`	To center the footer text on the page.
6 Save your changes and reload the page in Firefox	The footer text is centered on the page.
7 Add the following bold code to the nav rule: `nav { background-color: #f87217;` **`letter-spacing: 2px;`** `}`	
8 Save your changes and reload the page in Firefox	There are now two pixels of space between each text character in the `<nav>` element.
9 Close all open files	

Topic C: Box styles

Explanation

Every element in an HTML document creates a box. An inline element creates an inline box, and a block element creates a block box. This *box model* is the basic rendering model of CSS. The styles of the box model are those that directly influence the appearance of these boxes: height and width, borders, padding, and margins.

CSS borders

You can achieve a variety of design effects with CSS borders. You can give any rendered element a border, on any or all four sides of its box. An element's border is drawn around its content area and padding, as shown in Exhibit 3-5. *Padding* is the space between an element's content and its border.

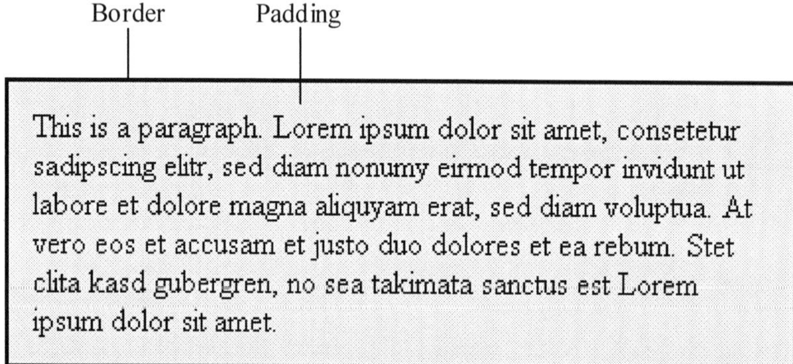

Exhibit 3-5: A solid border around a paragraph (with padding)

Borders are a popular design tool because they provide a way to visually separate content sections and they can draw a user's eye to a specific element.

Border properties

There are several border properties that you can use to set border width, style, and color. The following properties apply to all four sides of an elements' box: `border-color`, `border-width`, and `border-style`.

You can also determine which sides of an element you want a border to apply to by using the following properties: `border-left`, `border-right`, `border-top`, and `border-bottom`.

If you want one or more sides of an element's box to have different border styles, widths, or colors, you can use the following additional properties:

- `border-left-width`, `border-right-width`, `border-top-width`, and `border-bottom-width`
- `border-left-color`, `border-right-color`, `border-top-color`, and `border-bottom-color`
- `border-left-style`, `border-right-style`, `border-top-style`, and `border-bottom-style`

Border color and width

You apply a border color the same way you do with any other color specification—you can use color-name keywords, such as white, black, red, and green, or you can use hexadecimal values. (You can also use RGB notation.)

For best consistency among browsers and platforms, define border width values in pixels. To do this, use a positive integer, followed immediately by `px`. For example:

```
border-width: 2px
```

Border styles

There are several predefined border styles that you can apply to an element, as shown in Exhibit 3-6. The appearance of these border styles will vary slightly depending on the width of the border and the browser in use.

Solid	Groove
Double	Ridge
Dotted	Inset
Dashed	Outset

Exhibit 3-6: Border styles

A border's color can alter the appearance of its style. For example, the ridge effect is the result of slightly lighter and darker shades of the specified color, blended to create the illusion of outset, rounded lines. If the border color is too dark, the ridge effect will not be visible.

The border shorthand property

When you want to apply a border to all four sides of an element, use the `border` shorthand property. When you use the `border` property, you specify three values, which represent the border's width, style, and color. These values must be separated by a space. For example, the following rule gives all level-one headings a two-pixel, solid red border:

```
h1 { border: 2px solid red; }
```

This shorthand rule is the same as writing:

```
h1 { border-width: 2px;
     border-style: solid;
     border-color: red; }
```

It's more efficient to use the shorthand notation whenever possible. The order in which you enter these shorthand values is not important. The specific properties are implicit in their values. In other words, the following rule would create the same result:

```
h1 { border: solid red 2px; }
```

If you need to create a border on one or more individual sides, you can write:

```
h1 { border-left: 2px solid red;
     border-right: 2px solid red; }
```

This code will create borders on the left and right sides of the element. You can specify only the top border, the top and bottom borders, only the right border, and so on.

The none value

With border properties, you can specify `none` as a value to help keep your code as efficient as possible. For example, if you want an element to have a three-sided border, it's easier to set the full border and then disable one side, as follows:

```
h1 { border: 2px solid red;
     border-bottom: none; }
```

This is more efficient than writing the following equivalent rule:

```
h1 { border-left: 2px solid red;
     border-top: 2px solid red;
     border-right: 2px solid red; }
```

Do it!

C-1: Applying borders

The files for this activity are in Student Data folder **Unit 3\Topic C**.

Here's how	Here's why
1 In Firefox, open outlander.html	This page is already linked to an external style sheet. You'll continue to modify the page by using CSS styles.
2 In Notepad, open globalstyles.css	(From the styles folder, in the current topic folder.) You'll add more rules to this style sheet.
3 Add the following bold code to the h2 rule:	To apply a solid gray border on all four sides of every level-two heading.
`h2 { font-size: 18px;` **`border: 2px solid #ccc;`** `}`	
4 Save your changes and reload the page in Firefox	Company news Last updated 12/22/12 ISO certification Outlander Spices is now ISO 900 A note about our history By **Alan Garver**, President The level-two headings share the same border style.

5 Add the following bold code to the nav rule:

```
nav { background-color: #f87217;
      letter-spacing: 2px;
      border-bottom: 6px double #063; }
```

6 Save your changes and reload the page in Firefox

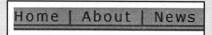

The navigation section now has a dark green double border on its bottom side.

7 Add the following bold code to the footer rule:

```
footer { font-size: 70%;
         text-align: center;
         border-top: 1px dashed #063; }
```

8 Save your changes and reload the page in Firefox

Contents © 2010-2015 Outlander Spices

(Scroll down to view the footer, if necessary.) The footer now has a thin, dashed border on its top side. In the next activity, you'll add padding to these elements to create space between the borders and the element content.

9 How can you use the `none` value to create a shorter equivalent of the following rule?

```
h1 { border-top: 2px solid red;
     border-bottom: 2px solid red;
     border-right: 2px solid red; }
```

Padding

Explanation

As mentioned before, an element's *padding* is the space between its content and its border. It's often important to add padding to elements that have borders because if text is too close to its borders, it can look unprofessional and detract from the readability of the content.

Applying padding

To apply padding, you use the `padding` property. This is a shorthand property, which includes the `padding-top`, `padding-right`, `padding-bottom`, and `padding-left` properties. For example, to apply 10 pixels of padding to all four sides of a footer element, you would write:

```
footer { padding: 10px; }
```

If you want to apply padding to only the top and bottom of the element, you can write:

```
footer { padding-top: 10px; padding-bottom: 10px; }
```

If you want to apply padding to each side except one—the top, for example—you can specify a value of zero for that side, as follows:

```
footer { padding: 10px; padding-top: 0; }
```

This is more efficient than writing out the left, right, and bottom padding properties and omitting the top padding property. You can also apply different padding values to each side of an element as needed. For example, you could write:

```
footer { padding-top: 8px; padding-bottom: 22px; }
```

Do it!

C-2: Applying padding

Here's how	Here's why
1 Switch to the style sheet	

2 Add the following bold code to the nav rule:
`nav { background-color: #f87217;`
`letter-spacing: 2px;`
`border-bottom: 6px double #063;`
`padding: 8px;` `}`	

3 Save your changes and reload the page in Firefox	 The nav section now has more space between the content and its borders. This has the effect of increasing the size of the element itself.

4 Add the following bold code to the nav rule:
`nav { background-color: #f87217;`
`letter-spacing: 2px;`
`border-bottom: 6px double #063;`
`padding: 8px;`
`padding-bottom: 0;` `}`
	To remove the padding from the bottom side only.

5 Save your changes and reload the page in Firefox	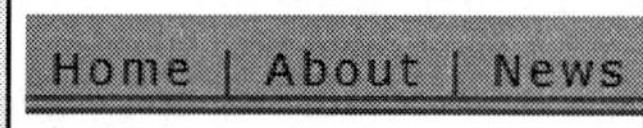 The padding has been removed from the bottom.

6 Add the following bold code to the h2 rule:
`h2 { font-size: 18px;`
`border: 2px solid #ccc;`
`padding: 5px;` `}`	

7 Save your changes and reload the page in Firefox	 Outlander Coffee a Company news Last updated 12/22/12 ISO certification Outlander Spices is now ISO 900 A note about our history The level-two headings now have more space between the content and the element borders.

8 Add the following bold code to the p rule:
 	
`p { line-height: 1.5;`
`text-align: justify;`
`padding-left: 20px;`
`padding-right: 20px;` `}`
	To give all paragraphs 20 pixels of padding on the left and right sides.

9 Save your changes and reload the page in Firefox	Paragraph text is now offset from the edges of the window.
10 Add the following bold code to the h3 rule: `h3 { font-size: 16px;` **`padding-left: 20px;`** `}`	To line up the heading with the paragraphs.
11 Add 20 pixels of padding to the footer rule	
Verify your results	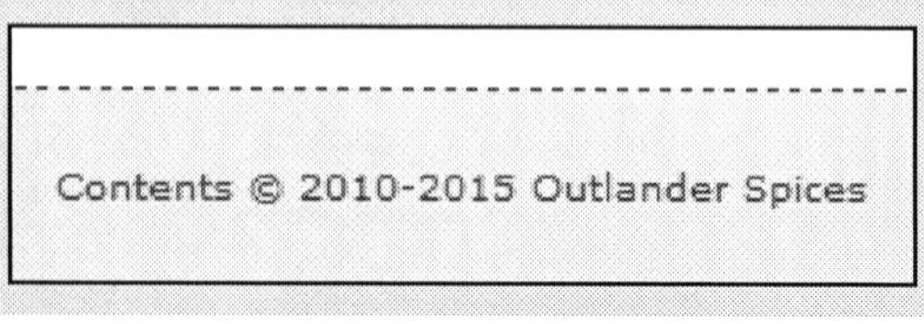 Contents © 2010-2015 Outlander Spices

Rounded corners

Explanation

You can use the `border-radius` property to create rounded borders. It's a shorthand property that applies the value to all four sides of an element. You can use it in conjunction with a border to create rounded border corners, as shown in Exhibit 3-7, or you can use it with a background color and no border styles to create a rounded background effect, as shown in Exhibit 3-8. Before this feature was supported, you had to use images to create such rounding effects, which led to the over-use of images and therefore less efficient documents that required more bandwidth.

```
border-radius: 20px;
border: 3px solid gray;
```

Exhibit 3-7: A rounded border

```
border-radius: 20px;
background-color: #ddd;
```

Exhibit 3-8: A rounded background color

The border-radius property

The `border-radius` shorthand property comprises the following individual properties, which you can use to create rounded corners individually: `border-top-left-radius`, `border-top-right-radius`, `border-bottom-left-radius`, and `border-bottom-right-radius`.

You can create a variety of rounding effects by using these properties. It can get more complicated than this, but at its most simple, the `border-radius` property works by applying the curvature of a sphere to each corner, as defined by the length of the sphere's radius. The *radius* of a sphere is the measure of a line segment from the center of the sphere to its perimeter, or exactly half of the diameter of the sphere.

For example, in Exhibit 3-9, the box corners are rounded equally by 40 pixels, which is the length of the radius of an imaginary sphere set against the corner of the box. Two values of 40px are shown because each individual radius property has two radius variables, the horizontal radius and the vertical radius. When you specify a single value, such as `border-radius: 40px`, the value applies to both the horizontal and vertical radius, as well as to all the other corners of the box.

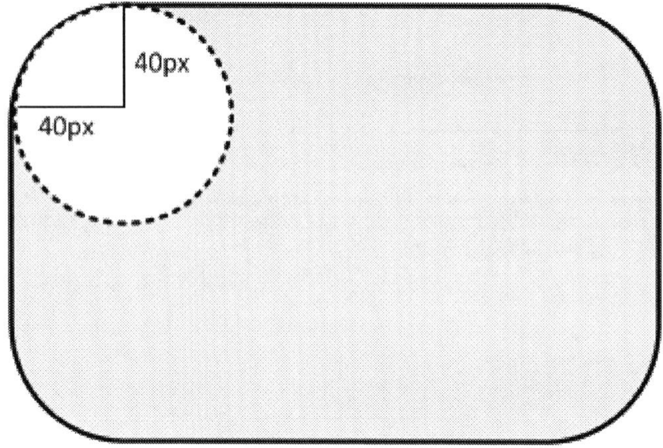

Exhibit 3-9: How border-radius is applied

Do it!

C-3: Creating rounded corners

Here's how	Here's why

1 Add the following bold code to the h2 rule:
`h2 { font-size: 18px;`
`border: 2px solid #ccc;`
`padding: 5px;`
`border-radius: 5px;` `}`
	To round the border edges slightly.

2 Save your changes and reload the page in Firefox	 Company news Last updated 12/22/12 ISO certification Outlander Spices is now ISO A note about our hist By **Alan Garver**, President The border edges of the level-two headings are now slightly rounded.
3 Change the border-radius value to **16px**	
4 Verify the result	 Company news Last updated 12/22/12 ISO certification Outlander Spices is now ISO A note about our hist By **Alan Garver**, President The borders are now rounded. How rounded a border looks can depend on the size of the element.

Box shadows

Explanation

Shadow effects are a popular design element that can add appeal and draw the user's eye to particular items. Until recently, shadow effects on Web pages had to be achieved with images. Now you can create shadow effects with CSS; these effects require less work to create and update. Using fewer images to achieve design objectives also helps to keep your pages lean and efficient.

The box-shadow property

The `box-shadow` property has a unique value system, in which you specify four values separated by spaces. As shown in Exhibit 3-10, the first value specifies the shadow's horizontal offset—a positive value offsets the shadow to the right of the element, and a negative value offsets the shadow to the left. The second value specifies the vertical offset—a positive value offsets the shadow from the bottom of the element, and a negative value offsets the shadow from the top. The third value specifies the distance of the shadow blur, and the fourth value specifies the shadow color.

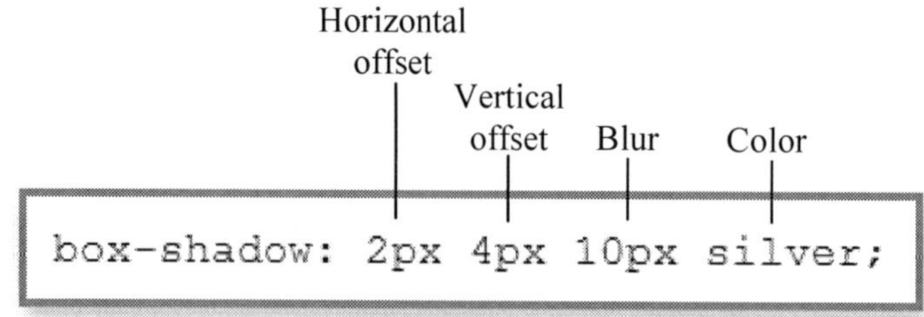

Exhibit 3-10: A box shadow effect and the code used to create it

Do it!

C-4: Creating a shadow effect

Here's how	Here's why
1 Add the following bold code to the h2 rule:	To apply a box shadow to level-two headings.

```
h2 { font-size: 18px;
     border: 2px solid #ccc;
     padding: 5px;
     border-radius: 16px;
     box-shadow: 4px 4px 4px gray; }
```

2 Verify the result	 The headings now have a shadow effect that makes them appear to be suspended above the page. This is just a simple example of the kinds of effects you can create.

Element dimensions

Explanation

You can control an element's dimensions (its height and width) by using the `height` and `width` properties. By default, a block element extends the full width of its parent element. If the parent element is the `<body>` element, the block will extend the full width of the page. In elements that contain paragraphs of text, line length is an important design consideration; excessive line length can make text difficult to read.

Controlling element width is also an important design technique that allows you to establish a specific page layout. If all elements on your page have a default width, your design and layout options are limited.

Fixed and flexible widths

To control an element's width, you use the `width` property. For example:

```
section { width: 500px }
```

This rules states that all `<section>` elements will be 500 pixels wide. Using a pixel value creates a *fixed width*, which means that the width will remain as specified, no matter how large or small the browser window might be.

You can apply a flexible width to an element by using a percentage value; for example:

```
section { width: 70% }
```

This rule will set the width of each `<section>` element to 70% of the width of its parent element. If the parent element is `<body>`, the section width will vary depending on the size of the user's browser window.

Element height

By default, the height of an element is determined by the size of the content it contains. You can use the `height` property to control the height of an element. For example, to give all `<header>` elements a fixed height of 50 pixels, you would write:

```
header { height: 50px; }
```

Applying styles by using element IDs

When you have an element with an ID, you can use that ID as a selector in your style sheet. This technique allows you to target styles to specific individual elements. Suppose that your pages are built with two `<section>` elements that define your content areas, and each section has its own unique ID:

```
<section id="mainContent">
Main content goes here...
</section>

<section id="archive">
Archive content goes here...
</section>
```

Instead of using `section` as a style selector, which will apply the style to all `<section>` elements, you can use an ID name as a selector to control the styles of only one unique element.

ID selectors begin with a number sign (#) followed by the ID name, with no space in between. For example, to make the text in the archive section navy blue, you would write:

```
#archive { color: navy; }
```

ID names are case-sensitive. Styles will not go into effect if the case in the HTML attribute and the case in the CSS rule are different. Also, an ID cannot begin with a number and must be unique to a document. That is, you can use an ID only once per document.

Using meaningful ID names

It's important to use meaningful ID names. Choose a name that describes the purpose of an element or the role it plays in the page structure—a name that will be meaningful to other developers who might need to read and modify the code. For example, ID names like "sidebar" and "footnote" provide meaning and context, while "areaB" and "coolSection" do not.

Do it!

C-5: Controlling element dimensions

The files for this activity are in Student Data folder **Unit 3\Topic C**.

Here's how	Here's why
1 In Notepad, open outlander.html	You'll add a new section, give it an ID, and then apply a style that uses the ID as a selector.
2 Directly below the `<nav>` element, add the following code: `<section id="content">`	To define the page's main content section. (The navigation section and footer are common to all pages, while the content section will vary from page to page.)
3 Scroll to the bottom of the file	
Directly above the `<footer>` element, close the new section	Type `</section>` to close the content section.
4 Switch to the style sheet	
5 Add the following rule: `#content { width: 80%; }`	
6 Save your changes and reload the page in Firefox	All page elements (except for the navigation section and the footer) now share the same width, which is equal to 80% of the browser's viewable area.
7 Resize the browser window	Because a percentage value was used to set the content section's width, the actual width varies based on the size of the browser window.
8 Switch to the style sheet	
Change 80% to **650px**	To apply a fixed width to the content section.
9 Save your changes and reload the page in Firefox	
Verify the result by resizing the browser window	The content section is fixed to a width of 650 pixels, so it's not affected by the size of the browser window. Depending on your design objectives, you might prefer this technique to a flexible width.

10 Add the following bold code to the nav rule:	To increase the height of the navigation section.

```
nav { background-color: #f87217;
      letter-spacing: 2px;
      border-bottom: 6px double #063;
      padding: 8px;
      padding-bottom: 0;
      height: 25px; }
```

11 Verify the result	The navigation section now has a fixed height of 25 pixels.

Margins

Explanation

You can control element spacing by applying margins. Every element creates a rectangular box. An element's *margin* is the space outside the boundaries of its box. Exhibit 3-11 shows sample text with padding and a thin, solid border. The margin is the amount of space outside the border, represented by the dark gray color.

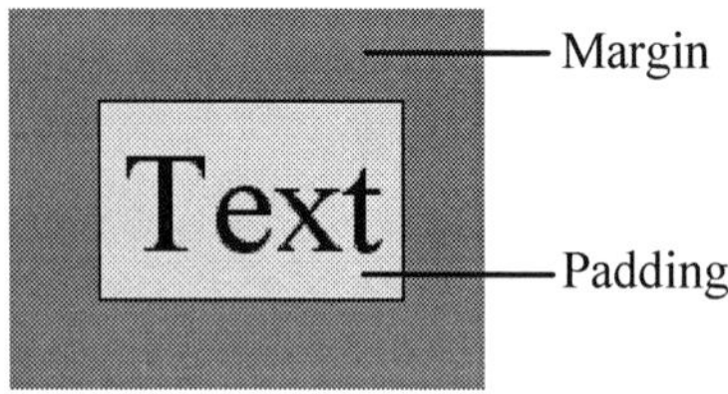

Exhibit 3-11: Margins and padding

Applying margins

To set margins, you can use the `margin` property. This is a shorthand property that consolidates four properties specific to each side: `margin-top`, `margin-right`, `margin-bottom`, and `margin-left`.

You can use these properties individually to set margins on specific sides, or you can use the `margin` shorthand property with a single value to apply the same value to all four sides. For example, to set a margin of 10 pixels on all four sides of every `<footer>` element, you would write:

```
footer { margin: 10px; }
```

Collapsing margins

When vertically adjacent elements have adjoining margin values, the margins collapse, meaning that the larger of the two values is used—the margin values are not summed.

In the following example, element A is above element B in the document flow. Element A has a margin of 20 pixels on all four sides of its box, and element B has a margin of 10 pixels on its four sides. The bottom margin of element A and the top margin of element B are adjoined, so they collapse. As a result, the total vertical margin between the two elements is the greater of the two adjoining margin values—20 pixels.

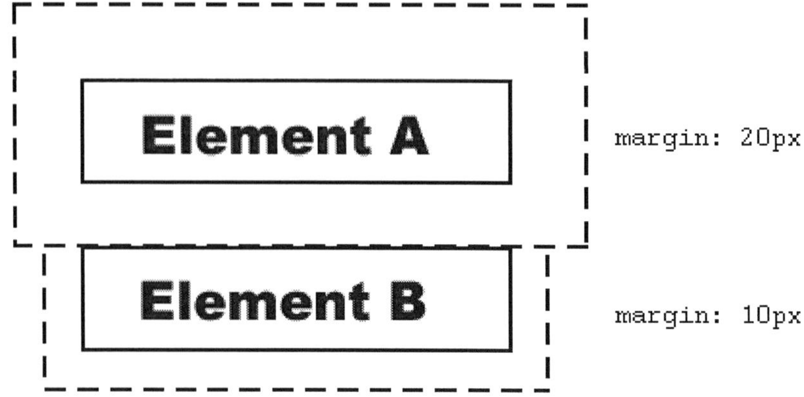

Exhibit 3-12: How elements with adjoining margin values are rendered

Clearing default margins

Browsers apply default margin values to many elements. For example, browsers give the `<body>` element a default margin of 8 pixels on all four sides, and give headings a top and bottom margin of about 20 pixels. These values can vary slightly depending on the browser.

You can clear a default margin by setting its value to zero. For example, the following rule removes the default margin that browsers give to all four sides of the `<body>` element:

```
body { margin: 0; }
```

Many developers routinely begin their style sheets with rules that reset the default values browsers give to certain elements. This technique gives the developer more control over the design and layout, and it ensures consistency across multiple browsers and platforms.

Do it!

C-6: Clearing and setting margins

Here's how	Here's why
1 In Firefox, observe the navigation section at the top of the page	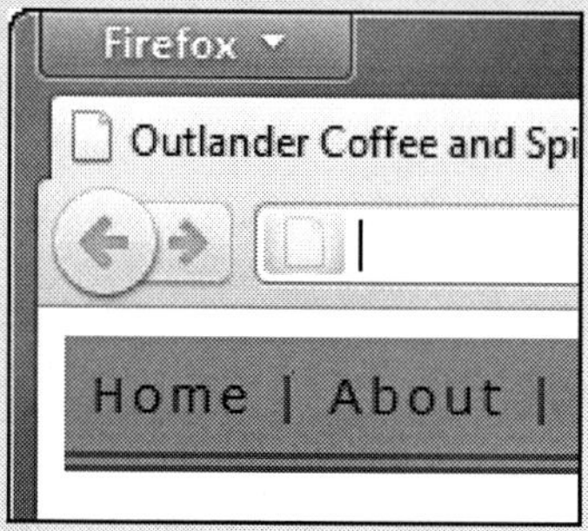 There's a default margin that creates space between page elements and the edges of the browser's viewing area. This default margin is applied to the `<body>` element.
Scroll down to view the footer	The default margin is on all four sides of the page.
2 Switch to the style sheet	
3 Add the following bold code to the body rule:	To clear the default margins that browsers give to all four sides of the body element.

```
body { font-family: Verdana, Geneva, sans-serif;
       font-size: 14px;
       margin: 0; }
```

Here's how	Here's why
4 Save your changes and reload the page in Firefox	Now, all the page content is flush against the edge of the browser's viewing area.
Scroll down to view the footer	The margin is cleared on all four sides.
5 Add the following bold code to the #content rule:	To apply a left margin of 25 pixels to the content section.

```
#content { width: 650px; margin-left: 25px; }
```

Here's how	Here's why
6 Verify the result	All the page elements inside the content section now have a left margin of 25 pixels. The navigation and footer sections remain flush against the edge of the browser window.
7 Add the following bold code to the p rule:	To clear the top margin for paragraphs.

```
p { line-height: 1.5;
    text-align: justify;
    padding-left: 20px;
    padding-right: 20px;
    margin-top: 0; }
```

8 Verify the result	The margin between paragraphs doesn't change because they also have a default bottom margin that is greater than zero. The greater of two adjoining margins is used.

9 Change the margin property as follows:
 	
`p { line-height: 1.5;`
`text-align: justify;`
`padding-left: 20px;`
`padding-right: 20px;`
`margin: 0;` `}`
	(Change margin-top to margin, and keep the same value.) To set both the top and bottom margins to zero.

10 Verify the result	Now the rule clears both the top and bottom default margins given to paragraphs, so there's no spacing between them.
11 Delete the margin style in the p rule	To return to the default paragraph margins.

Automatic margins

Explanation

A popular design technique is to use automatic (auto) margins to center page content. This is not the same as centering text, which is done by using the `text-align` property. Instead, automatic margins create an entire page "wrapper" that contains all your content. This effect ensures that your content is centered in a user's browser regardless of the size of the browser window.

Centering a content section

When you apply *auto margins* (also called *auto-width* margins) to the left and right sides of an element, the computed values of the two margins are equal. Therefore, when an element's left and right margins are equal, that element must be centered inside its parent element.

For example, if you have a `<section id="content">` element whose parent is the `<body>` element, you can center the content section on the page by using auto margins, as follows:

```
#content { margin-left: auto; margin-right: auto; }
```

The <div> element

Before browsers supported the new structural elements in HTML5, the `<div>` element was used to define all page sections and other containers. For example:

```
<div id="footer">
  All contents &copy; 2010-2020 XYZ Corp.
</div>
```

Now this kind of code is better handled with the `<footer>` element.

The lack of semantically meaningful structural elements prior to HTML5 resulted in pages made up of so many `<div>` tags that document structures became cluttered. In large documents, it was often difficult to determine which closing tag corresponded to which opening tag.

The `<div>` element, which is short for *division*, is a generic container that you can use when no semantically meaningful elements are appropriate. In other words, if you need to create a container that is not a section, article, footer, or any other self-describing element, you can use the `<div>` element. (It's typically used to create containers for layout purposes.)

Do it!

C-7: Centering a page by using auto margins

Here's how	Here's why
1 In Notepad, switch to outlander.html	
2 Directly after the `<body>` element, add the following code: `<div id="page">`	To start a <div> container that serves as a page wrapper for styling purposes only.
3 Scroll to the bottom of the file	

4 Directly above the closing body tag, add the following code: `</div>`	To close the "page" container.
5 Save your changes	
Switch to the style sheet	
6 Add the following bold code to the body rule:	To give the body element a gray background.

```
body { font-family: Verdana, Geneva, sans-serif;
       font-size: 14px;
       margin: 0;
       background-color: #ccc; }
```

	You'll apply a different background color to the new "page" element.
7 Add the following new rule:	

```
#page { border-left: 4px solid black;
        border-right: 4px solid black;
        width: 700px;
        background-color: white; }
```

8 Save your changes and reload the page in Firefox	The new "page" container can be distinguished by its different background color.
Resize the browser window so that you can see at least a couple inches of gray background	(If necessary.) Next, you'll center the "page" container in the browser window.
9 Switch to the style sheet	
Add the following bold code to the #page rule:	

```
#page { border-left: 4px solid black;
        border-right: 4px solid black;
        width: 700px;
        background-color: white;
        margin-left: auto; margin-right: auto; }
```

10 Verify the result	The "page" container is now centered in the browser window because the auto values force both left and right margins to be equal.
Resize the browser window	At any window size, the page is centered.
Return the browser to your preferred size	If necessary.

The <aside> element

Explanation

You can use the <aside> element to define content that is peripherally related to its adjacent content—that is, content that provides ancillary information for a main article or content region. For example, you can use the <aside> element to define a container for a *pull quote* (a quotation culled from an adjacent article) or to create a container for links that support a main article.

Floating an element to the left or right

You can use the `float` property to arrange an element to the left or right of adjacent content. For example, the gray box in Exhibit 3-13 is an <aside> element that's floated to the left, forcing adjacent content to wrap around the other side. To successfully float an element, you typically need to give it a specific width so that content can wrap around it. You should also give it a margin to create space between it and the adjacent content.

Using the <aside> element, you could use the following CSS rule to create the example shown in Exhibit 3-13:

```
aside { float: left; font-size: 120%;
        margin-right: 20px; padding: 12px;
        background-color: silver; width: 250px; }
```

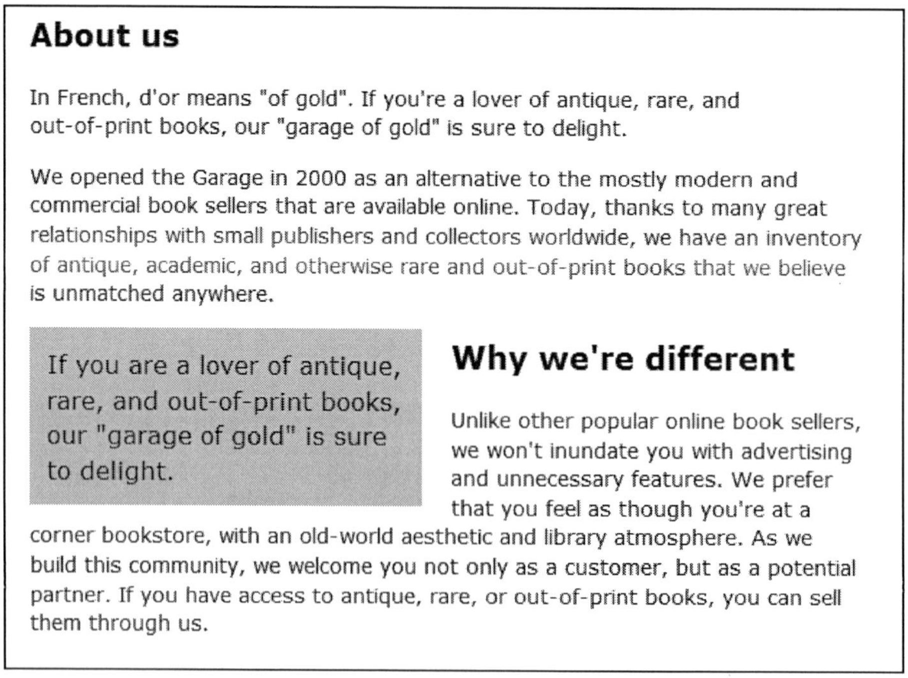

About us

In French, d'or means "of gold". If you're a lover of antique, rare, and out-of-print books, our "garage of gold" is sure to delight.

We opened the Garage in 2000 as an alternative to the mostly modern and commercial book sellers that are available online. Today, thanks to many great relationships with small publishers and collectors worldwide, we have an inventory of antique, academic, and otherwise rare and out-of-print books that we believe is unmatched anywhere.

If you are a lover of antique, rare, and out-of-print books, our "garage of gold" is sure to delight.

Why we're different

Unlike other popular online book sellers, we won't inundate you with advertising and unnecessary features. We prefer that you feel as though you're at a corner bookstore, with an old-world aesthetic and library atmosphere. As we build this community, we welcome you not only as a customer, but as a potential partner. If you have access to antique, rare, or out-of-print books, you can sell them through us.

Exhibit 3-13: An element floated to one side of its adjacent content

Do it!

C-8: Floating an element

Here's how	Here's why
1 In Notepad, switch to outlander.html	
Locate the block quote	Scroll down, if necessary.
2 Wrap the block quote in an `<aside>` element, as shown:	

```
<aside>
<blockquote>
"As always, only the best will do, for you and all our
partners worldwide."
</blockquote>
</aside>
```

Here's how	Here's why
3 Save and close outlander.html	
Switch to the style sheet	
4 Add the following rule:	

```
aside { float: right; width: 280px;
        margin: 20px; border-radius: 30px;
        background-color: #9c9; }
```

Here's how	Here's why
5 Save and close the style sheet	
6 Reload the page in Firefox	(screenshot below)

Outlander Coffee and Spices opened its doors in 1989 as a wholesale provider of coffee and spices from around the world. Today, we're one of the largest coffee and spice wholesalers in the country. A few years ago we expanded into retail, opening three stores that quickly exeeded our expectations and sales forecasts.

"As always, only the best will do, for you and all our partners worldwide."

In a recent study published in the trade publication *Global Trader*, analysts found that "U.S. spice imports hit a record high last year, the strongest year-over-year results since record-keeping began in 1966." Supported by this trend, we will continue to expand in the United States in the coming months and years, starting in Boulder, Colorado and Austin, Texas.

We hope that you will explore an Outlander store near you. I encourage you to participate in the Outlander Club™. As a frequent customer, you will receive a club card that entitles you to 5% off all purchases. **If you register by March 2, 2012, you will receive 10% off all purchases for the remainder of the year.**

The `<aside>` element is floated to the right of the adjacent content, which wraps around the opposite side.

7 Close all open files

Unit summary: Style sheets

Topic A

In this topic, you learned how to use **style sheets** to format HTML content. You learned how to write **CSS rules**, embed a style sheet in a document, and create an external style sheet and link documents to it. You also learned about **hexadecimal color values** and you applied colors and background colors. You also learned about the **cascade**, or how CSS styles are resolved when conflicts occur.

Topic B

In this topic, you learned how to apply basic text and font styles. You learned how to set the **font** and **font size** for elements, and you learned about the difference between serif and sans serif fonts. You also learned how to control **line height**, letter spacing, and text alignment.

Topic C

In this topic, you learned about **box styles**. You learned how to apply borders and padding, create **rounded corners** and **shadows**, control element dimensions, and create both fixed and flexible widths. You also learned how to apply styles to an ID, control **margins**, clear default margins, and center a page by using automatic margins. Finally, you learned how to **float** an element to the left or right of adjacent content.

Independent practice activity

In this activity, you will link pages to an external style sheet and add style rules to format the pages. You will apply text and font styles, apply background colors, and set the width, borders, margins, and padding for elements.

The files for this activity are in Student Data folder **Unit 3\Unit summary**.

1 In Firefox, open about-gdb.html.

2 In Notepad, open styles.css (from the styles folder in the current Unit summary folder).

3 In Notepad, open about-gdb.html.

4 Link the .html file to the styles.css style sheet.

5 In the style sheet, create a rule that sets the default font to **Verdana, Helvetica, sans-serif** at a font size of **12px**. (*Hint:* Apply the style to the `<body>` element.)

6 Save the style sheet and reload the page in Firefox to verify your changes.

7 Create a rule that gives level-one headings a font size of **22px**.

8 Create a rule that gives level-two headings a font size of **16px**.

9 Set the line height of all paragraphs to **1.5**.

10 Create a rule for the `<nav>` element that includes the following styles:

- **10** pixels of padding on all four sides
- The background color value **#69C** (a pale blue)
- **2** pixels of letter spacing

11 Apply the same styles in the preceding step to the `<footer>` element. (*Hint:* Add **footer** as another selector in the same rule.)

12 Verify your changes.

13 In the page's HTML, between the opening and closing body tags, add a `<div>` element with the ID **page**. In the style sheet, create a rule that gives this element the following styles: (*Hint:* Use **#page** as the selector.)

- A width of **725px**
- Left and right automatic margins
- Left and right border values of **12px solid #369**
- A **white** background color
- A border radius of **10px**

14 Between the `<nav>` and `<footer>` elements, add a `<div>` element with the ID **content**. In the style sheet, create a rule that gives this element the following styles:

- A width of **600px**
- A left margin of **15px**

15 Add the following additional styles to the body rule:

- The light gray background color **#ddd**
- A margin value of **0**

16 Verify your changes. Compare your results to Exhibit 3-14.

17 Close all open files.

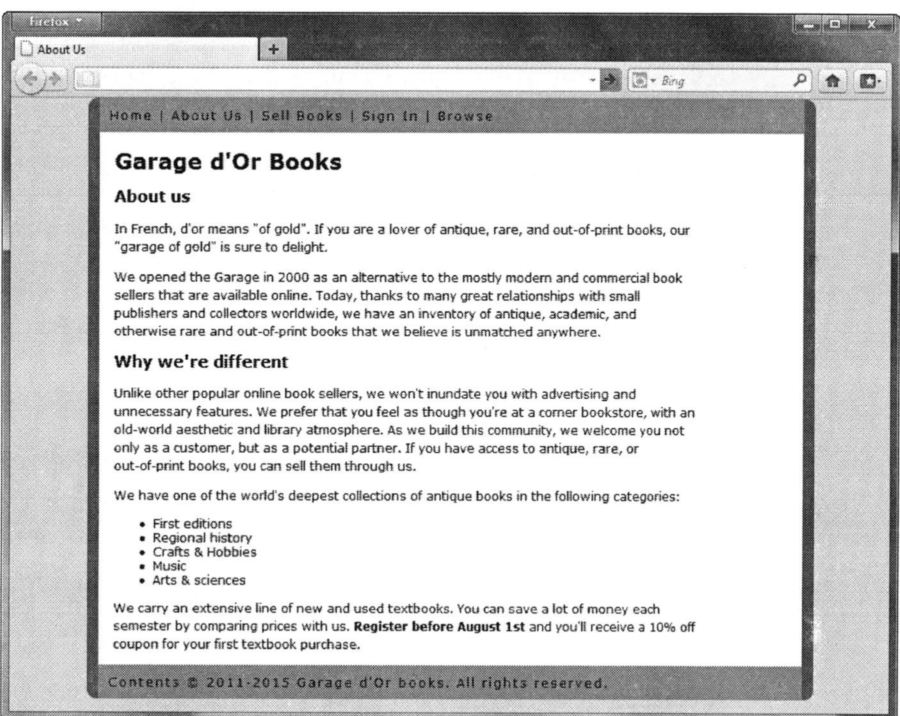

Exhibit 3-14: The completed page

Review questions

1 What is an external style sheet?

2 When is it appropriate to use an embedded style sheet?

3 What is the shorthand value for the hexadecimal color #CC9933?

4 True or false? A page can be linked to multiple external style sheets.

5 What does the "cascading" part of Cascading Style Sheets refer to?

6 What is padding?

A The space outside an element's border

B The space between an element's content and its border

C An element's border size

D The space between letters

7 What two properties can you use to control an element's dimensions?

8 When should you use the `<div>` element to contain content?

9 Which of the following best describes an element's margin?

A The space between an element's content and its border

B The space to the left and right of an element

C The space outside the boundaries of the element's box

D The spacing inside an element

10 What property do you use to control the spacing between adjacent lines of text?

11 If a heading has a bottom margin of 20 pixels, and a paragraph that follows it has a top margin of 25 pixels, how much space will there be between the heading and the paragraph?

A 25 pixels

B 20 pixels

C 45 pixels

D 0 pixels

12 Which of the following statements are true? [Choose all that apply.]

A ID names are case-sensitive.

B An ID name cannot begin with a number.

C Styles that use an ID selector must be in an external style sheet, not an embedded style sheet.

D An ID can be used only once per HTML document.

Unit 4
Tables

Unit time: 45 minutes

Complete this unit, and you'll know how to:

A Create and modify tables, apply styles to tables, and define table headers and footers.

Topic A: Displaying tabular data

Explanation

Tables can be an effective way to organize and display certain types of information. For example, a list of products and their prices is typically best displayed in a table because a table structures the data in a familiar and intuitive format.

HTML tables

As shown in Exhibit 4-1, an HTML table is a grid of rows and columns meant to display data of various types. Data is contained in cells, similar to the cells in a spreadsheet.

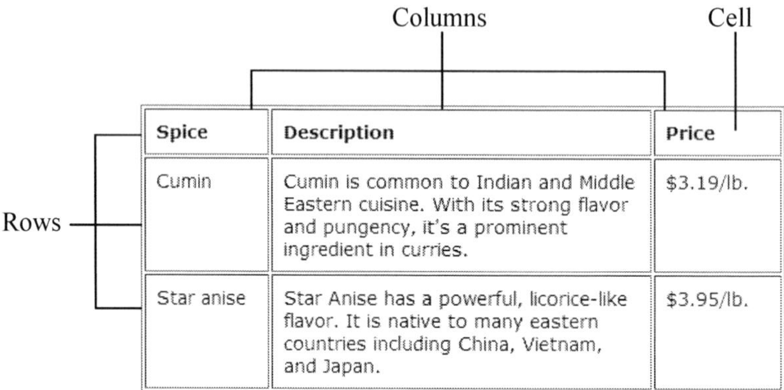

Spice	Description	Price
Cumin	Cumin is common to Indian and Middle Eastern cuisine. With its strong flavor and pungency, it's a prominent ingredient in curries.	$3.19/lb.
Star anise	Star Anise has a powerful, licorice-like flavor. It is native to many eastern countries including China, Vietnam, and Japan.	$3.95/lb.

Exhibit 4-1: Tables consist of rows, columns, and individual cells

Minimally, a table consists of the following elements:

Element	Description
`<table>` `</table>`	Defines a table and contains all other table elements and content.
`<tr>` `</tr>`	Stands for "table row." This element does not directly contain content. Each instance of the `<tr>` element creates a row, and each row contains one or more `<td>` elements, which contain the content.
`<td>` `</td>`	Stands for "table data." Each `<td>` element creates a column and contains the table content.
`<th>` `</th>`	Stands for "table header." It functions the same as the `<td>` element but is meant to define and contain headers that briefly describe the data.

By default, tables are displayed without borders. You can specify a border for a table by using the `border` attribute, but this method is discouraged in HTML5 in favor of using CSS border styles. While you're creating a table, it can be helpful to use borders so that you can see the gridlines, which allow you to distinguish between rows and columns and more easily find and correct errors. So, you can use the `border` attribute so you can see the table as you're building it, remove the attribute when you're done, and then apply CSS border styles if necessary.

The following code produces the simple table shown in Exhibit 4-2:

```
<table border>

 <tr>
  <th>Product Name</th>
  <th>Price</th>
 </tr>

 <tr>
  <td>Green Cardamom</td>
  <td>$3.99</td>
 </tr>

</table>
```

Product Name	Price
Green Cardamom	$3.99

Exhibit 4-2: A simple two-row, two-column table

Table headers

Table headers are defined by the `<th>` element and should be used only to provide information about row or column data. For instance, in Exhibit 4-2, the Product Name and Price headers describe their column data. By default, content in a `<th>` element is bold and centered in its cell.

Do it!

A-1: Creating a table

The files for this activity are in Student Data folder **Unit 4\Topic A**.

Here's how	Here's why
1 In Firefox, open specials.html	This page contains some new styles and several spice names and descriptions. You'll create a table to display the products and corresponding prices.
2 In Notepad, open specials.html	
3 Under "September specials," type the following bold code: `<h2>September specials</h2>` **`<table>`** **`<tr>`**	To start a table and a table row.
4 Put "Coriander" in a `<td>` element, as follows: **`<td>`** `Coriander` **`</td>`**	
5 Wrap the Coriander description in another `<td>` element	The spice descriptions will be in a second column of cells.
On the next line, close the row	Insert a `</tr>` tag after the cell containing the Coriander paragraph.

Verify that your code is the same as shown	`<table>`
	`<tr>`
	`<td>`
	`Coriander`
	`</td>`
	
	`<td>`
	`<p>`
	`Coriander has a mild`
	`the Middle East, and`
	`in curries, while the`
	`Mexican dishes.`
	`</p>`
	`</td>`
	`</tr>`

6 Above “Cinnamon,” start a new row

Insert a <tr> tag.

Put “Cinnamon” and its paragraph in separate cells, and close the row

```
<tr>
<td>
Cinnamon
</td>

<td>
<p>
Cinnamon is one of ou
goods and candies. Ci
two kinds of cinnamon
predominant variety b
aroma. <i>Ceylon</i>
flavor than Cassia.
</p>
</td>
</tr>
```

7 Do the same for Cumin, as shown

```
<tr>
<td>
Cumin
</td>

<td>
<p>
Cumin is common t
and pungency, it'
</p>
</td>
</tr>
```

8 Do the same for the last two spices, as shown

```
<tr>
<td>
Cloves
</td>
<td>
<p>
Cloves are dried
natively in Madag
even medicine dat
aroma and are com
</p>
</td>
</tr>

<tr>
<td>
Turmeric
</td>
<td>
<p>
Turmeric comes fr
family. The root
common in Indian
</p>
</td>
</tr>
```

9 On the next line, close the table

Insert a </table> tag after the last closing table-row tag.

10 Save your changes and reload the page in Firefox

September specials

Coriander	Coriander has a mild Asia, the Middle East, common in curries, w Mexican dishes.
Cinnamon	Cinnamon is one of c baked goods and canc There are two kinds o predominant variety b aroma. *Ceylon* cinnam than Cassia.

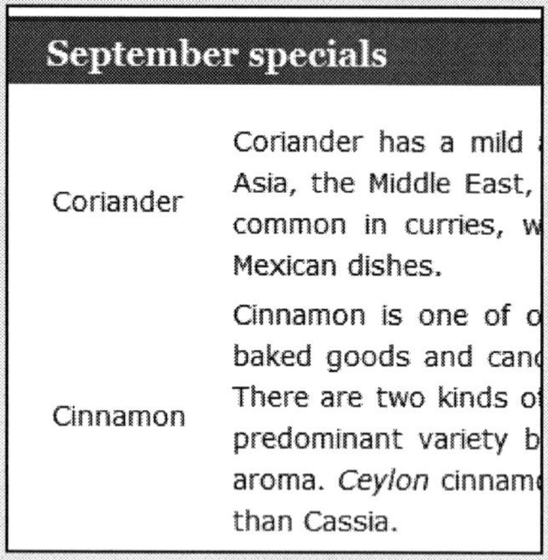

The spice names and their descriptions appear in different columns. Notice that by default, tables do not have borders.

11 Switch to Notepad and add the following bold code to the table:

```
<table border>
```

To show the table gridlines. Using this attribute temporarily while you create a table can help you see the row and columns better and find any errors that might exist. To control table borders properly, you should use CSS border styles.

Verify the result

(Save your changes and reload the page in Firefox.) A border now appears, showing the gridlines of the table rows and columns.

12 After the opening table tag, add the following bold code:

```
<table border>

<tr>
<th>Product</th>
<th>Price</th>
<th>Description</th>
</tr>
```

To create a new row for table headers. This code will create three new columns.

13 Verify the result

A new row, with three columns, appears at the top of the table. By default, the text in the <th> elements is bold and centered in the cells. You can change this default style with CSS.

Observe the Price column

The column header does not match the information in the column because the header row contains three columns and the rest of the table has only two.

14 After the Coriander cell, enter the following code:

```
<td>
$12.99/lb
</td>
```

Put the new cell between the Coriander cell and the cell that contains the description.

15 Select the new cell, as shown

```
<tr>
<td>
Coriander
</td>

<td>
$12.99/lb
</td>


<td>
<p>
Coriander has a m
the Middle East,
in curries, while
Mexican dishes.
</p>
</td>
</tr>
```

Press CTRL + C

To copy the code.

16 Paste the code after each spice-name cell

To give every spice a price data cell.

17 Change the price of cinnamon and cumin to **$9.99/lb**

18 Compare your results to the section of the table shown here

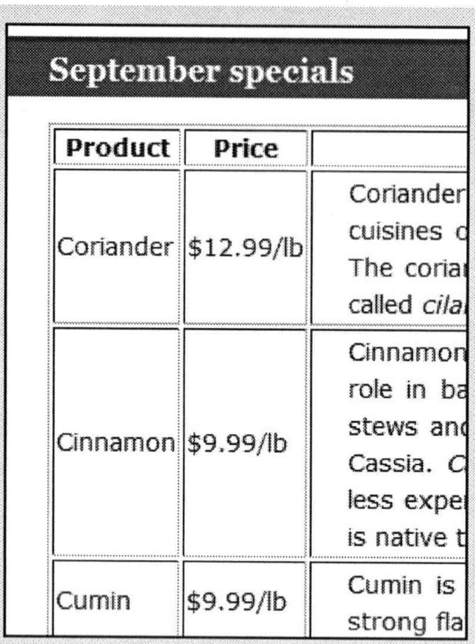

September specials

Product	Price	
Coriander	$12.99/lb	Coriander cuisines c The coria called *cila*
Cinnamon	$9.99/lb	Cinnamon role in ba stews and Cassia. *C* less expe is native t
Cumin	$9.99/lb	Cumin is strong fla

Observe the height of the rows

By default, the height of a row is determined by the amount of content in that row. The Cinnamon row is taller than the Cumin row because its description has more content, and the cell stretches to accommodate the content.

Observe the location of the spice names in their cells

The height of each cell in a table row is equal and determined by the largest cell in that row. By default, content is vertically centered in its cell; this alignment can result in row content that is not vertically aligned. In the next activity, you'll align the spice names to the top of their cells.

Formatting table elements

Explanation

Previous versions of HTML included several attributes for table formatting. HTML5 does not include these older attributes because the better way to apply formatting is to use a CSS style sheet. Using a style sheet offers far greater control over various aspects of design, and it keeps your HTML lean and free of unnecessary code. Of course, using styles sheets also makes it possible to update the styles of multiple pages by changing only one CSS file.

Table width

To control the width of a table, you use the `width` property, the same as you would to control the width of any other element. For example, to give a table a width that is 90% of the width of its parent element, you would write:

```
table { width: 90%; }
```

Vertical alignment

By default, content is vertically centered in table cells. If a cell has a larger height than its content requires, the content will be centered, and this can result in row content that is not equally aligned. To control vertical alignment by using a style sheet, you use the `vertical-align` property. The value options are `top`, `middle`, and `bottom`.

For example, to vertically align the content in all table cells to the top of each cell, you would write:

```
td { vertical-align: top; }
```

The `vertical-align` property applies only to content in table cells and to images that are inline with text.

Do it!

A-2: Applying table styles

The files for this activity are in Student Data folder **Unit 4\Topic A**.

Here's how	Here's why
1 Open globalstyles.css	(From the styles folder, in the current topic folder.) You'll use this style sheet to format the table.
Scroll to the end of the style sheet	You'll add new style rules to format the table.
2 Add the following rule: `table { width: 600px; font-size: 90%; }`	
3 Save the style sheet and reload the page in Firefox	To view the result. The table is now 90% of the width of its parent element, which is the page container indicated by the white background. The text size in the table is now 90% of its inherited value.
4 Add the following rule: `th { text-align: left; }`	
5 View the result	(Save the style sheet and reload the page in Firefox.) The headers are now left-aligned in their cells.

6 Add the following rule:
`td, th { padding: 5px;`
`vertical-align: top; }`	

7 View the result	The table cells now have the same amount of padding, and the content is consistently aligned to the top of each cell.
Observe the spice descriptions	The style sheet contains a rule that gives all paragraphs extra padding on the left and right sides. This style carries through to paragraphs in the table.
8 In the HTML, remove the **border** attribute from the `<table>` tag	
View the result	The table gridlines are no longer shown. In the next activity, you'll apply CSS border styles.

Using row groups to refine a table's structure

Explanation

To clarify your table structure and target CSS styles more specifically, you can use the following elements: `<thead>`, `<tbody>`, and `<tfoot>`. Each of these elements defines one *row group*:

- `<thead>` — Defines a row or group of rows that comprise the column headings.
- `<tbody>` — Defines a group of rows that comprise the table's data.
- `<tfoot>` — Defines a row or group of rows that comprise the table's footer.

Each row group must contain at least one row, which means that it must have one or more `<tr>` elements. All three row group elements should have the same number of columns.

The `<tfoot>` element can precede the `<tbody>` element in the code. With this technique, browsers can load the header and footer first, while the table data loads. This placement is optional, but it can be beneficial with large tables, especially those that depend on server processing to output many rows of data.

The `<thead>`, `<tbody>`, and `<tfoot>` elements do not replace the `<tr>`, `<td>`, and `<th>` tags. Rather, you use them together to create a better, more meaningful table structure.

Advantages of defining row groups

There are many advantages of defining row groups:

- You can use `thead`, `tfoot`, and `tbody` as selectors in a style sheet.
- Defining row groups can make your table code easier to read and understand. This is particularly helpful if you work in a team, and other developers need to review or modify the code.
- When a large table is printed and divided into multiple pages, the table's header and footer content is repeated on each page, providing important context.
- Defining row groups makes it possible to create a scrollable `<tbody>` section while the header and footer rows remain fixed in place.

In addition, browsers that don't support these elements ignore them and display the remaining table code normally, so there's no real disadvantage to using them.

Do it!

A-3: Defining row groups

Here's how	Here's why
1 In the HTML, locate the row containing the column headers	

Add the following bold code around the header row:
`<table>`
`<thead>`
`<tr>`
`<th>Product</th>`
`<th>Price</th>`
`<th>Description</th>`
`</tr>`
`</thead>`
	To define the header row.

2 On the next line, enter the following code and text:
`<tfoot>`
`<tr>`
`<td>Our special offers are updated monthly. Prices are the same for both whole and ground spices.`
`</td>`
`</tr>`
`</tfoot>`
	(After the closing thead tag.) To define a footer.
	
	Placing the footer before the body of the table allows the footer information to load before the table data is finished loading.

3 On the next line, after the closing table footer tag, type **<tbody>**	To start the body of the table.
4 Directly above the closing table tag, type **</tbody>**	(Scroll down in the code to find the `</table>` tag.) To close the table body.
5 Verify the result	(Scroll to view the footer, if necessary.) The footer text is confined to the first cell in its row because only one cell was added to the row. You'll make this row span all three columns in the next activity.

Spanning rows and columns

Explanation

You can extend rows or columns so that they span adjacent rows or columns. This technique allows you create customized arrangements of data, headers, and footers.

Spanning columns

If you want a cell to span two or more columns, use the `colspan` attribute in that cell to specify the number of columns to span. For example, the header row shown in Exhibit 4-3 spans all three columns in the table. To achieve this, you would use one `<th>` element that spans three columns, as follows:

```
<th colspan="3">Products and their prices</th>
```

The `colspan` and `rowspan` attributes are valid only in `<td>` and `<th>` tags. They are not valid in a `<tr>` tag.

Products and their prices		
Product	Net Weight	Price
Green cardamom	4 oz.	$3.99
Chilies	4 oz.	$4.99

Exhibit 4-3: A cell spanning three columns

When you span rows or columns, the number of rows or columns you specify must include the cell in which the `rowspan` or `colspan` attribute is placed. Make sure that the total number of spanned columns, plus the remaining columns, equals the total number of columns in the table. The same principle is true for spanning rows.

Controlling font weight

The boldness of text is referred to as a font's *weight*. To make an element bold without having to use the `<b>` tag in your HTML, you can use the `font-weight` property in a style sheet. Possible values include `bold`, `bolder`, and `lighter`. For example, to make the text in `<tfoot>` elements bold, you would write:

```
tfoot { font-weight: bold; }
```

You can also specify integer values from 100 to 900, but these values depend upon the font in use, and results are inconsistent.

Do it!

A-4: Spanning columns

Here's how	Here's why
1 In the table footer, add the following bold code:	To allow the cell in the footer row to span all three columns in the table.

```
<tfoot>
<tr>
<td colspan="3">Our specials are updated monthly. Prices
include both whole and ground spices.
</td>
</tr>
</tfoot>
```

Here's how	Here's why
2 Verify the result	Now the footer content spans all three table columns. Notice that the footer appears at the bottom of the table, even though it was entered after the headings in the code.
3 Switch to the style sheet	
4 Add the following rule:	

```
thead,tfoot { background-color: #eee;
              font-weight: bold; }
```

Here's how	Here's why
	The styles will apply to both the header and footer rows.
5 Verify the result	The table header and footer share the same styles.
6 Close all open files	

Unit summary: Tables

Topic A

In this topic, you learned how to create and modify **tables** to display tabular data. You learned how to define a **table structure** by using the <thead>, <tbody>, and <tfoot> elements, and you learned how to apply **styles** to table elements. Finally, you learned how to **span** rows and columns to arrange data, headers, and footers.

Independent practice activity

In this activity, you'll create and modify a table, add a header and footer, and apply CSS styles.

The files for this activity are in Student Data folder **Unit 4\Unit summary**.

1 In Firefox, open gdb.html.

2 In Notepad, open gdb.html.

3 Create the table and text shown in Exhibit 4-4, using the following specifications:

- Create the table in the "main" section, and display table borders so you can see the gridlines while you work. (Be sure to close the table before the closing section tag.)
- In the first row, use `<th>` elements to define the headers.
- Wrap the header row in a `<thead>` element.
- After the table header, start a `<tfoot>` element that contains the footer row shown at the bottom of the table. Make the footer row span all three columns.
- After you close the table footer, wrap the remaining rows in a `<tbody>` element. (Be sure to close it before the closing table tag.)

4 In Notepad, open styles.css (from the styles folder).

5 Modify the table as shown in Exhibit 4-5, using the following styles:

- Set the table width to **500px**.
- Left-align all text in the table. (*Hint:* Add the style to the same table rule you used to set the width.)
- Apply 10 pixels of padding to both table header cells and normal data cells. (*Hint:* Use **th, td** as the style selector.)
- Apply the background color value **#eee** to the table header and footer. (*Hint:* Use **thead, tfoot** as the style selector.)

6 Verify the results and make any necessary modifications.

7 Close all open files.

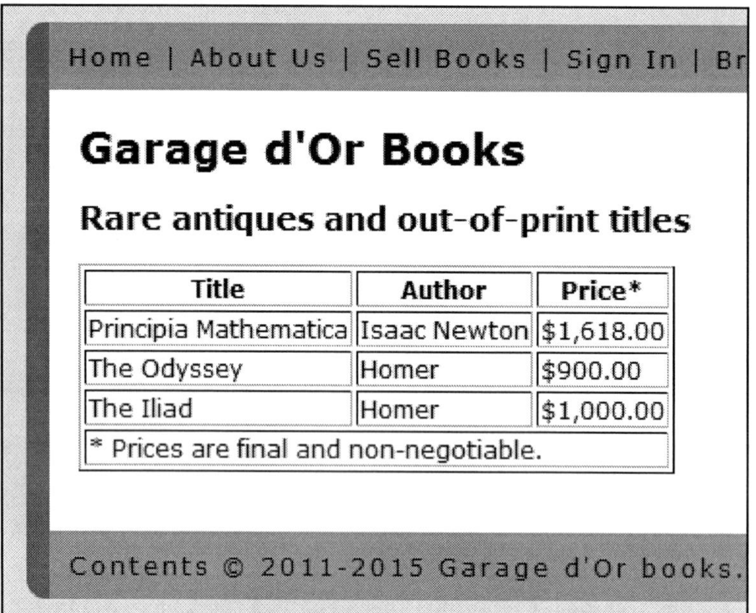

Exhibit 4-4: The table after Step 3

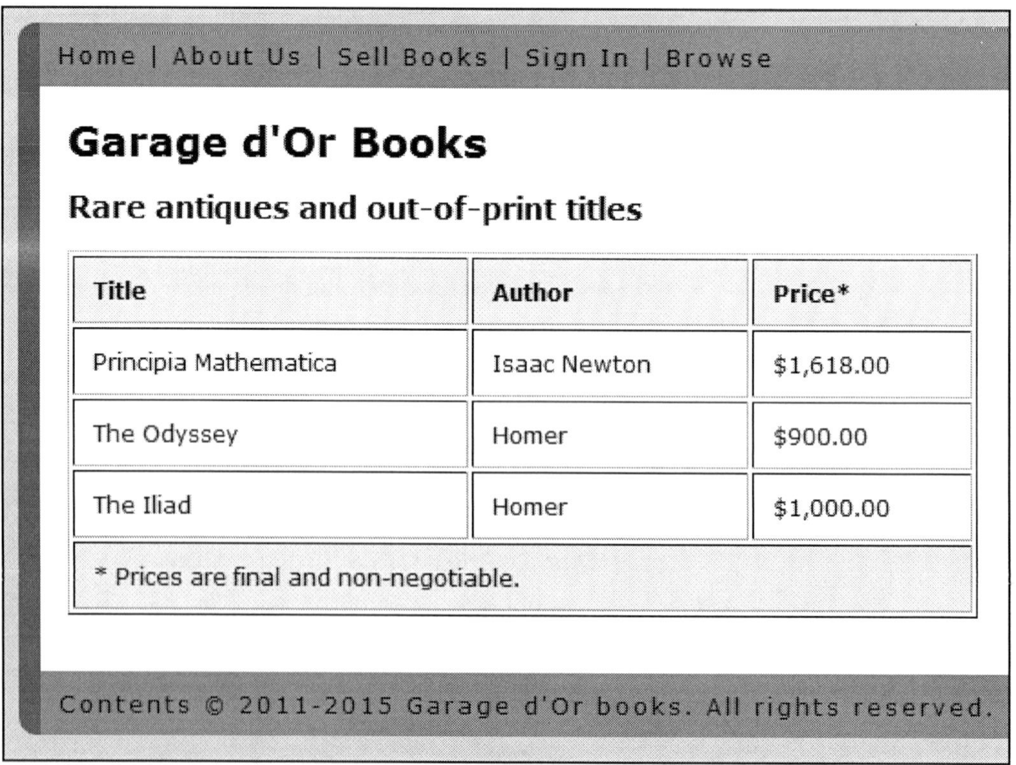

Exhibit 4-5: The completed table

Review questions

1 Which three elements are used to define row groups?

2 True or false? Table headers (`<th>` elements) should be used to contain information about row or column data.

3 Which of the following CSS rules will align content to the top of each table cell?

A `table { vertical-align: top; }`

B `table { align: top; }`

C `td { align: top; }`

D `td { vertical-align: top;}`

4 True or false? The `<tfoot>` element can precede the `<tbody>` element in the HTML code.

5 True or false? The `colspan` and `rowspan` attributes are valid only in `<td>` and `<th>` tags. They are not valid in a `<tr>` tag.

Unit 5

Links and images

Unit time: 60 minutes

Complete this unit, and you'll know how to:

A Create internal and external links, format links using CSS, and apply styles contextually.

B Identify different image formats, embed images, write effective text alternatives, and apply background images.

Topic A: Creating and formatting links

Explanation

Hyperlinks, or links, as they're more commonly called, allow you to connect two or more Web pages together. One reason the Web is such an effective network of information is that users can move from one page or site to another quickly and easily. For example, a Web site usually has a series of consistent links on every page so that users can easily navigate to each page or category of information in the site.

The <a> element

You use the `<a>` element (also called the *anchor* tag) to create a link. Any text inside an `<a>` element will be a link that a user can click to navigate to the specified page or resource. The `href` attribute (hypertext reference) of the `<a>` element specifies the address or file name of the destination page. The syntax for a link is as follows:

```
<a href="URL or filename of page">Text that serves as link</a>
```

For example, to link to another page of your site that's in the same directory (folder) as the current page, you could write:

```
<a href="mypage.html">Text that serves as link</a>
```

If the page that you're linking to is in another folder, you need to specify the folder name first, followed by a forward slash, and then the file name of the destination page, for example:

```
<a href="sales/info.html">Text that serves as link</a>
```

Default link styles

By default, browsers make link text blue and underlined, and links that you have visited will be purple and underlined. You can change these default styles by using CSS.

Do it!

A-1: Creating links

The files for this activity are in Student Data folder **Unit 5\Topic A**.

Here's how	Here's why
1 In Firefox, open index.html	This is the Outlander Spices home page. Index.html is a common file name for a site's home page.
2 In Notepad, open index.html	Right-click the file and choose Open with, Notepad.
3 Locate the nav section, as shown	<nav id="siteNav"> Home | About | News </nav>
4 Add the following bold code around the word "Home": **`<a href="index.html">`**`Home`**`</a>`**	To create a link. In this case, clicking the link would reload the home page.
5 Add the following bold code around "About": **`<a href="about.html">`**`About`**`</a>`**	To make the text "About" a link to the about.html page.
6 Make "News" a link to news.html	
7 Make "Specials" a link to specials.html	
8 Make "Recipes" a link to recipes.html	
9 Save your changes and reload the page in Firefox	By default, the links are blue and underlined, and the Home link is purple because it has been visited (it's the current page). Browsers apply these default styles to links and visited links; you can use CSS to create custom link styles.
10 Click **About**	The about.html page opens. This and all the other pages already have the same navigation links that you created previously.
Click **News**	To open the news.html page. Notice that as you visit each link, it changes to purple in the navigation bar.
11 In Notepad, close index.html	

Linking to external resources

Explanation

You can also create links to other Web sites. For example, to link to Microsoft's Web site, you would write:

```
<a href="http://www.microsoft.com">Microsoft's Web site</a>
```

Here, the `href` attribute specifies the full address of the destination page. This address is called a *URL*, which is an abbreviation for Uniform Resource Locator. When a user clicks this link, the browser leaves the current site and opens Microsoft's home page.

Opening links in a new browser session

By default, browsers open links in the current browser session. If you want to provide links to external resources without forcing users to lose their place on your site, you can set the link to open in a new browser session (or on a new tab, depending on the browser). To do this, add a `target` attribute with the value `"_blank"` to the anchor tag. For example:

```
<a href="URL of external site" target="_blank">link text</a>
```

Note that the value begins with the underscore character, followed by the keyword `blank`.

Do it!

A-2: Making a link open in a new browser session

The files for this activity are in Student Data folder **Unit 5\Topic A**.

Here's how	Here's why
1 In Notepad, open news.html	You'll create a link to an external Web site and make it open in a new browser session.
2 Locate the ISO 9000 text	(In the first paragraph.) The abbreviation ISO is in an `<abbr>` element.
3 Make "ISO 9000" a link to **http://www.iso.org**	Start the anchor tag before the `<abbr>` element.
4 Save your changes and reload the page in Firefox	The text "ISO 9000" is now a link.
Click **ISO 9000**	The ISO Web site opens in the current browser window.
In Firefox, go back to news.html	(Click the left-pointing arrow on the Firefox toolbar.) You'll modify the link.
5 Switch to Notepad and add the following bold code to the link: `<a href="http://www.iso.org" target="_blank">`	
6 Save your changes and reload the page in Firefox	
Click **ISO 9000**	The ISO Web site now opens in a new tab.
Close the ISO site tab	To return to the news.html page.
7 In Notepad, close news.html	

Link styles

Explanation

You can change the default styles of links to fit your site's color scheme and to provide visual cues about the state of the links. Effective link styles can add a unique design touch and improve the overall user experience.

Link states

Every link has four possible *states*, or link conditions, which are defined by user activity. Here they are:

- The *default state* is the normal state of a link whose destination has not yet been visited.
- The *hover state* is activated when you point to a link.
- The *active state* is the usually brief moment between the clicking of a link and the release of the mouse button that ends the clicking process.
- A link enters the *visited state* when it destination page or resource has already been visited. The link itself does not necessarily have to have been clicked to appear in its visited state.

As mentioned earlier, links appear as blue, underlined text by default, and visited links are purple and underlined. You can change these default styles by targeting the `<a>` element in your style sheet. In addition, you can apply styles to each link state.

Pseudo-class selectors

To apply styles to a link state, you use a *pseudo-class selector* in the style sheet. These selectors begin with the element name (in this case, `a`) followed by a colon (:) and then the state name, as follows:

- Using `a:link` as your style selector applies the included styles to links in their default state.
- Using `a:hover` as your style selector applies the included styles to a link only when a user points to that link.
- Using `a:active` as your style selector applies the included styles to a link only in the moment when it's clicked and before the mouse button is released.
- Using `a:visited` as your style selector applies the included styles only to links that have already been visited.

For example, if you want all your links to be navy blue by default, gray when they've been visited, and red when the user points to them, you can add these rules to your style sheet:

```
a:link { color: navy; }
a:visited { color: gray; }
a:hover { color: red; }
```

The order of these rules is important. An `a:visited` rule should precede an `a:hover` rule. Otherwise, the hover effect won't work on any link that has already been visited.

The text-decoration property

You can control the underlining of text by using the `text-decoration` property. Possible values are `underline`, `overline`, `line-through`, and `none`. So, if you want to remove the default underlining for links, write this:

```
a:link { text-decoration: none; }
```

Do it!

A-3: Applying link styles

The files for this activity are in Student Data folder **Unit 5\Topic A**.

Here's how	Here's why
1 In Notepad, open globalstyles.css	(From the styles folder in the current topic folder.) You'll add link styles to this style sheet.
2 Scroll to the bottom	
On an empty line, write the following rule:	
`a:link { color: black; font-weight: bold; text-decoration: none; }`	
3 Save your changes and reload the page in Firefox	By default, all links now have no underlining and their text is bold. Unvisited links are black, but visited links remain purple because they have their own default color style. To override the purple style, you need to create a rule that uses `a:visited` as the selector.
4 On the next line, write the following rule:	To make visited links dark gray.
`a:visited { color: #555; }`	
Verify the result	Now, all visited links are dark gray, and they continue to inherit the bold and no-underline styles from the `a:link` rule.
5 On the next line, write the following rule:	To make link text dark red with a white background when a user points to it.
`a:hover { color: #930; background-color: white; }`	
6 Save your changes and reload the page in Firefox	
Point to the navigation links	When you point to a link, its text color changes to a dark red and the background color changes to white, which has the effect of highlighting the link.
Point to the **ISO 9000** link	The link text changes color. There's no apparent change in the background color because it's already white.

Styling elements based on their context in the document

Explanation

In addition to using element names, IDs, and class names as selectors, you can apply styles to elements in a particular context in the document. For example, you might want to apply certain styles to links only if those links are inside a `<nav>` element. Applying styles based on an element's context can help keep your code lean because you don't have to introduce new class or ID names to the element you want to format.

Contextual selectors

To apply styles to elements that are used in a particular context, you use *contextual selectors* (also known as *descendent selectors*). The syntax of a contextual selector is:

```
parentElement targetElement { property: value; }
```

For example:

```
footer p { font-size: 11px; }
```

The leftmost selector is the parent element—the context for the element you're targeting. The two selectors must be separated by a space.

In plain English, this rule states, "give only those paragraphs that are inside a `<footer>` element a font size of 11 pixels." This technique promotes efficiency because you don't have to introduce any new code in the HTML, as you would with a class or ID style.

You can also specify multiple levels of context. For example, you could write:

```
footer p em { font-weight: bold; }
```

This rule states, "make any `<em>` element bold if it's inside a paragraph that's inside a `<footer>` element."

Do it!

A-4: Applying styles based on element context

Here's how	Here's why
1 On the next line in the style sheet, write the following rule: `nav a { padding: 8px; }`	To give only those links inside a <nav> element an extra 8 pixels of padding.
2 Save the style sheet and reload the page in Firefox	There's now extra space between the links in the navigation section.
Point to the navigation links	The additional padding widens the background color area, producing a fuller highlight effect.
3 Observe the ISO 9000 link	No additional padding is applied to this link because it's not inside the <nav> element.
4 Add the following rule: `nav a:hover { color: black; }`	
5 Save the style sheet and reload the page in Firefox	
Point to the navigation links	The text stays black when you point to these links.
Point to the **ISO 9000** link	Links that are not inside a <nav> element are dark red when you point to them.
6 Close all open files	

Topic B: Working with images

Explanation

You can embed images to add design elements and functionality to your pages. You can also use CSS to add background images; this can be a more efficient solution than embedding images directly in the HTML code.

Image formats

There are three image formats commonly used on the Web: GIF, JPG, and PNG. For optimal image quality and file size, it's important to use the correct file format when creating an image for the Web.

GIF images

Graphic Interlaced Format, or *GIF*, is an image format for non-photographic images that contain a small number of colors or areas of solid color. For example, the logo in Exhibit 5-1 is a typical GIF image. GIF images have a .gif file extension, as in OutlanderLogo.gif.

GIF is not the best format for photographs because it's limited to 256 colors. Most photographs will look distorted if saved as GIF files.

Exhibit 5-1: A GIF image

JPG images

JPG (or JPEG) stands for *Joint Photographic Experts Group*. This file format can include over 16 million colors, so it's optimized for photographic images. JPG images have a .jpg file extension, as in Photograph1.jpg.

PNG images

PNG (commonly pronounced "ping") stands for *Portable Network Graphics*. This format was introduced to improve upon the GIF format in terms of transparency options and color depth. It supports 16 million colors, but like GIF, the PNG format is not optimized for photographic images.

Creating images

To create any of these types of images, you need to use an image editing program such as Photoshop, Fireworks, or Paint Shop Pro. These programs make it easy to create graphics for use on your Web pages.

Do it!

B-1: Discussing image file formats

Questions and answers

1 As the Web designer at Outlander Coffee & Spices, you want to add a high-quality photograph of every spice available on the Products page. Which image format is probably best for these images?

2 The following image is best saved in what image format?

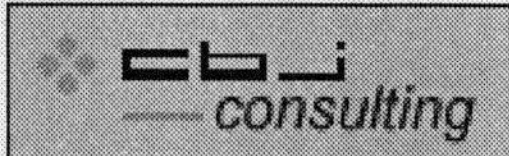

3 Which format is probably best for a complex drawing that contains areas of solid color and thousands of colors and gradients?

The <img> element

Explanation

To embed an image in a page, you use the <img> element. You use the `src` attribute to specify the path and file name of the image file. For example:

```
<img src="images/MyImage.gif">
```

This example will embed the image MyImage.gif in the location in which the element appears in the code. The <img> element is an empty element, so it does not have a closing tag. If you're following XHTML authoring guidelines, you must include a terminating slash at the end of the tag, as follows:

```
<img src="images/house.jpg" />
```

If you're using the more loose HTML authoring requirements, you can omit the terminating slash.

Relative and absolute paths

The previous examples of the <img> element use a relative path to the image file. A *relative path* refers to the location of a file relative to the page being viewed. In this case, the forward slash (/) indicates that the images folder is a subfolder of the folder in which the current page is stored.

You can also specify an absolute path to an image or other external file. An *absolute path* is the complete URL to a file. For example:

```
<img src="http://www.outlanderspices.com/images/logo.gif" />
```

Specifying image height and width

The <img> element is one of only a few elements that still allow the use of formatting-related attributes. You can include `height` and `width` attributes to specify an image's dimensions. Doing so allows the browser to create a "placeholder" for the image, so other content can load while the image file loads. For example:

```
<img src="images/image.gif" width="120" height="200" />
```

The numerical values represent pixels: 120 pixels wide and 200 pixels high. You can use Windows Explorer to determine the height and width of your image. Simply point to the image file, and a ScreenTip appears, showing the dimensions of the image.

File storage

It's important to organize your site's resources into distinct folders, organized by type or purpose. For example, you should store your image files in a separate folder, just as you would with resources like style sheets, scripts, and video files. You should also name each folder according to the resources they contain, e.g., images, scripts, styles, and so on.

Do it!

B-2: Embedding images

The files for this activity are in Student Data folder **Unit 5\Topic B**.

Here's how	Here's why
1 In the current topic folder, open the images folder	The folder contains two images: one GIF file and one JPG file.
Point to **outlander.gif**	A ScreenTip appears, showing the dimensions of the image: 660 x 34 pixels.
2 Navigate back to the current topic folder	
In Firefox, open index.html	
In Notepad, open index.html	
3 Below the `<div id="page">` element, write the following code:	To embed the outlander.gif image at this location in the document.
`<img src="images/outlander.gif" width="660" height="34" />`	
Save and verify your changes	 The image appears above the navigation bar. The image and the "page" container have the same width, 660 pixels.
4 Select the top-level heading, as shown	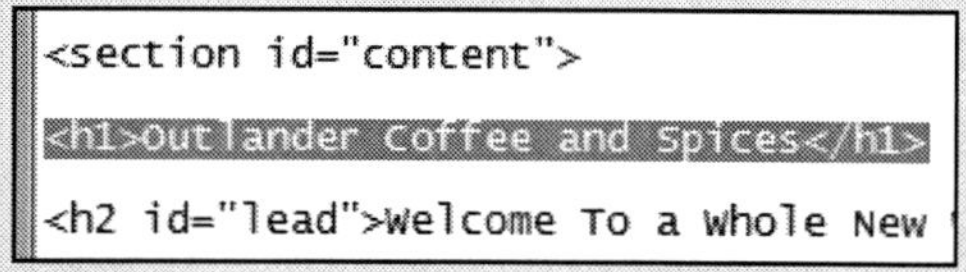 `<section id="content">` `<h1>Outlander Coffee and Spices</h1>` `<h2 id="lead">Welcome To a Whole New`
Press DELETE	To delete the heading. The logo now provides the site identity.

5 On the same line, write the following code:

```
<img src="images/spices.jpg" width="660" height="103" />
```

Save and verify your changes

The image serves as a design-oriented header.

Providing text alternatives

Explanation

It's important to include a text alternative for each instance of an embedded image so that site visitors who have visual impairments and use non-visual browsers, such as screen readers, can know what the image shows or understand its context in the document. A text alternative (often called "alt text") can be a description of a photographic image, as in "Sunset over New York," a simple indication of the purpose of the image, as in "Outlander Spices logo," or text that precisely duplicates the text that appears in the image.

To specify a text alternative for an embedded image, you use the `alt` attribute. For example:

```
<img src="images/logo.gif" alt="XYZ Company Logo">
```

When a screen reader encounters this image, it will read aloud the text alternative, providing the user with information and context.

Instructive, descriptive, and replacement text

Depending on the nature of the image, there are several ways you can communicate the information in, or the purpose of, an image. Suppose that a page contains two images, which act as "previous" and "next" links for navigating through an online help system. If these images do not have a text alternative, and a user with a screen reader tries to use this help system, the user might get lost or confused because there would be no indication that the images provide a means of navigation. To improve the usability of the page, you could specify instructive text for the images. For example:

```
<img src="previous.gif" alt="Go to the previous page." />
```

Instructive text should clearly indicate an action that the user should or can take. *Descriptive text* should describe the content of the image. For example, if you have a picture of an ocean view, your text alternative might read "Picture of an ocean view" or "View from Virginia Beach."

Finally, use *replacement text* when your image contains text that you want the user to read. Screen readers and other non-visual browsers cannot access text that's inside an image, so it's up to you to ensure that users can access the same content. For example, if you have a GIF image that reads "BeeHive Record Company," your text alternative should literally replace this content—it should read "BeeHive Record Company."

Text alternatives improve usability and accessibility

Providing text alternatives will help all users, not just users with visual impairments. Alternative text will appear in place of an image if the user has disabled images in the browser or if the images fail to download. Another benefit of writing effective text alternatives is that search engines can access the text. They can't access the content in an image file or determine the purpose of an image without this important information. Therefore, providing effective text alternatives can lead to better search results.

Use proper punctuation in your text alternatives

If your text alternative is a complete sentence, use proper punctuation. Screen readers use punctuation to emulate the natural pauses and inflections in speech.

Do it!

B-3: Writing effective text alternatives

Here's how	Here's why
1 In the HTML, locate the outlander.gif image	
Add the following bold code to the `<img>` tag:	

```
<img src="images/outlander.gif" width="660" height="34" ▶
alt="Outlander Spices logo" />
```

Here's how	Here's why
	To specify a text alternative that both describes the purpose of the image and replaces the text inside the image.
2 Write appropriate alt text for the "spices" image	
3 Is your text alternative best defined as replacement text, descriptive text, or instructive text?	
4 Save your changes in index.html	

Use background images for design efficiency

Explanation

When an image is part of your site-wide design, it's typically best to apply it as a background image instead of an embedded image. For example, if you want to use the same image on multiple pages to achieve a particular design effect, you can use CSS to make it an element's background image, instead of using an image tag in every page.

Even if this requires adding a new element to attach the background image, the element will still require less code than a properly written image tag. More important, you can change the image in the style sheet to update the background image for every page simultaneously. If you ever need to update your design, which is practically inevitable, this technique could save you a significant amount of time and effort.

Applying background images

There are several CSS properties you can use to apply and control background images. You can attach background images to an entire page or to specific page elements. For example, suppose you want to create an element named "banner" that you want to use to alternate design-oriented images once per week on all the pages in your Web site. You could write:

```
<div id="banner"></div>
```

With this empty container in place, you can attach a background image to it and control its display characteristics.

The background-image property

To attach a background image, you use the `background-image` property. The syntax of this property is unique in that the value requires `url`, followed immediately by parentheses that enclose the path and file name of the image, as follows:

```
#banner { background-image: url(images/banner1.gif); }
```

Any background image that you apply to an element will repeat until the dimensions of the element are filled up. This repeating is also called "tiling." You can force a background image not to repeat or to repeat in only one of two directions (vertically or horizontally).

The background-repeat property

To control the tiling of a background image, you use the `background-repeat` property. There are four possible values: `repeat` (the default value); `no-repeat`, which turns off the repetition; `repeat-x`, which repeats the image horizontally; and `repeat-y`, which repeats the image vertically. For example, if you want a background image to repeat only vertically, you can write:

```
#banner { background-image: url(images/banner1.gif);
          background-repeat: repeat-y; }
```

Writing resource paths in a style sheet

The path that you write to an image, or to any external resource, is critical. If the path isn't correct, you'll get bad results. If you're accustomed to embedding images in your HTML, you know that a path such as `images/myImage.gif` works if the image is stored in a folder named "images."

However, if you declare an image from an external style sheet, the style sheet is not located in the same folder as the document in which you want the image to appear. Most likely, you'll store the style sheet in a "styles" folder or some other aptly named folder. Therefore, your path will need to first escape out of the styles folder before it can specify the folder where the image is stored. To do this, the code would be:

```
#banner { background-image: url(../images/banner1.gif); }
```

The path to the image begins with `../`, which tells the browser to look "up one level" in the folder structure. Depending on how you organize your site folders, you might need to escape out of multiple folders.

Specifying the dimensions of a background image

If the element to which you are applying a background image does not contain any content, and it does not have height and width settings, then you won't be able to see the background image because the element will have no size—there will be no "window" through which to view the background image.

If the element does contain text content, but does not have a height or width setting, then the size of the image will be defined by the amount of content the element contains. This could result in a partial view of the background image, which might not be the result you want. Therefore, it's important that you always specify either a height or width value, or both, depending on the situation. To do this, you use the `height` and `width` properties, as follows:

```
#banner { background-image: url(../images/banner1.gif);
          height: 300px; width: 200px; }
```

Do it!

B-4: Applying background images

The files for this activity are in Student Data folder **Unit 5\Topic B**.

Here's how	Here's why
1 In the HTML, select the image tag for the Outlander logo, as shown	`<div id="page">` `<img src="images/outlander.gif" logo" />` `<nav id="siteNav">`
Press DELETE	To delete the image. You'll apply the same image as an element background for better control and document efficiency.
2 In the same location, enter: `<div id="logo"></div>`	You'll make the logo image a background of this empty container.
Save your changes	
3 From the styles folder, open globalstyles.css	In the current topic folder.
Scroll to the bottom of the style sheet	
Add the following rule: `#logo { background-image: url(../images/outlander.gif); }`	
4 Save the style sheet and reload the page in Firefox	(Index.html should be open in Firefox.) The logo image is not visible because the "logo" element contains no content, and therefore has no height through which to view the background image.
5 Switch to the style sheet	
Add the following bold code to the `#logo` rule: `#logo { background-image: url(../images/outlander.gif);` **`height: 34px;`** `}`	To give the "logo" div container a height value equal to the height of the logo image.
Save the style sheet and view the results	The logo image appears in the same location as it did before, but now the image can be controlled from the style sheet.
6 Click the links to the other pages in the Web site	The other pages all share the background image because they all have the "logo" element already inserted at the same location.

	Step	Notes
7	Why is it unnecessary to specify a width for the “logo” element?	
8	In Firefox, click **Home**	To go back to the index.html page, if necessary.
9	Switch to index.html	
	Delete the other image tag	(Under the “content” section.) You’ll create another empty container.
10	In the same location, type:	
	`<div id="spiceBanner"></div>`	
	Save your changes	
11	Switch to the style sheet	
	After the last rule, create the following new rule:	

```
#spiceBanner { background-image: url(../images/spices.jpg);
               height: 103px; }
```

	Step	Notes
	Save the style sheet	
12	Reload the page in Firefox	The spice image appears in the same location as before.
	Verify the result on the other pages	The other pages already contain the “spiceBanner” container.
13	What makes this method more efficient than embedding the image in each page?	
14	Is this method the right solution for all images you might use?	
15	Close all open files	

Unit summary: Links and images

Topic A

In this topic, you learned how to create **links**, make a link open in a new browser session, apply styles to various **link states**, and apply styles to elements based on their context in the document structure.

Topic B

In this topic, you learned about the three **image file formats** in use on the Web: GIF, JPG, and PNG. You learned how to embed an image, specify **image dimensions**, and write effective **text alternatives**. Finally, you learned how to apply **background images** from a style sheet for better efficiency when working with images that are common to multiple pages.

Independent practice activity

In this activity, you'll create and format links, embed an image, provide alt text, and use CSS to align the image to the right of the content area.

The files for this activity are in Student Data folder **Unit 5\Unit summary**.

1 Open index.html in Firefox and Notepad.

2 For the text Home, About Us, and Browse Titles, create links to index.html, about-us.html, and titles.html, respectively.

3 Between the two paragraphs, embed the image **almanac.jpg** (in the images folder). Include an appropriate text alternative for the image.

4 Open styles.css (from the styles folder).

5 Turn off the default underlining of links. (*Hint:* Use **a:link** as the selector, and use the **text-decoration** property.)

6 Apply the color value **#660** to the default state of links. (*Hint:* Add the color property to the existing a:link rule.)

7 Make visited links white.

8 Apply the color value **#930** to links in the hover state.

9 Use a contextual selector to align the almanac image to the right of the text content. (*Hint:* Use **#main img** as the selector, and **float: right** as the property and value.)

10 Compare your results to Exhibit 5-2.

11 Save and close all open files.

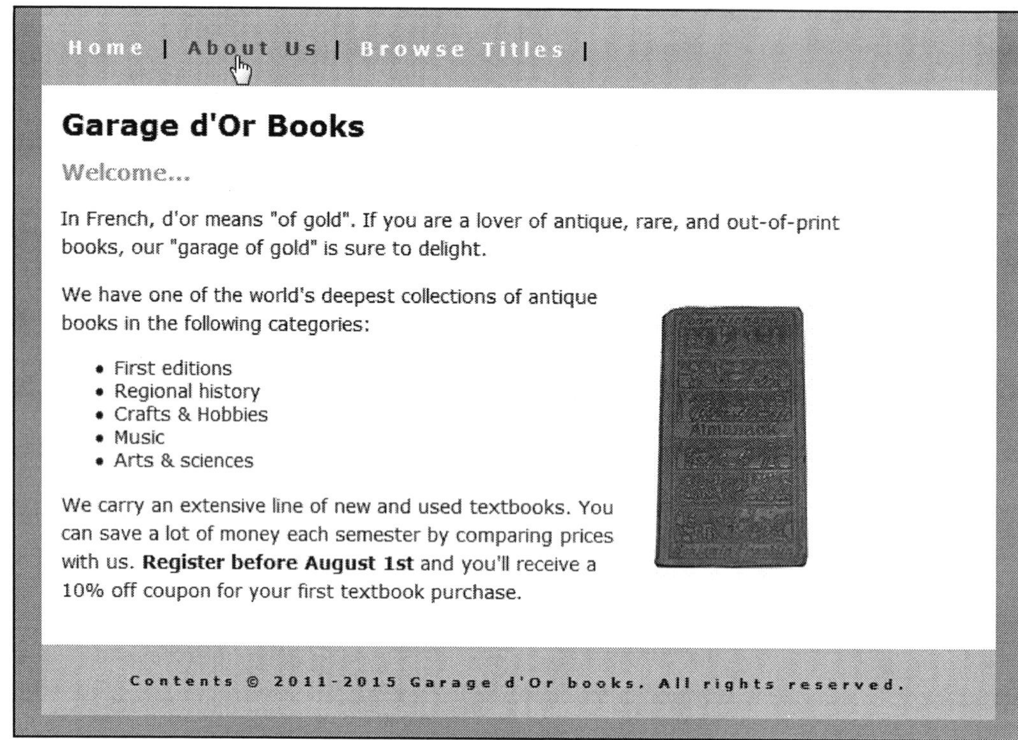

Exhibit 5-2: The completed page

Review questions

1 You want to embed an image named myImage.png on a page in your site. The image is stored in an "images" folder, which itself is stored in a "resources" folder. What will the `<img>` tag look like?

A `<img src="images/resources/myImage.png" />`

B `<img src="resources/images/myImage.png" />`

C `<img href="resources/images/myImage.png" />`

D `<img href="images/resources/myImage.png" />`

2 If you want a link to open in a new browser window, what attribute and value would you add to your link tag?

A `open="new"`

B `href="_blank"`

C `target="_blank"`

D `src="new"`

3 True or false? An `a:visited` rule should precede an `a:hover` rule in a style sheet; otherwise, the hover effect won't work on any link that has already been visited.

4 If you want to apply a gray background to only those blockquote elements that are inside an article, what will the rule look like?

A `blockquote article { background-color: gray; }`

B `article, blockquote { background-color: gray; }`

C `blockquote, article { background-color: gray; }`

D `article blockquote { background-color: gray; }`

5 Which image format is typically best only for photographic images?

A GIF

B Transparent GIF

C JPG

D PNG

6 Why is it important to always include a text alternative for each instance of an embedded image?

Course summary

This summary contains information to help you bring the course to a successful conclusion. Using this information, you will be able to:

A Use the summary text to reinforce what you've learned in class.

B Determine the next courses in this series (if any), as well as any other resources that might help you continue to learn about HTML5.

Topic A: Course summary

Use the following summary text to reinforce what you've learned in class.

Unit summaries

Unit 1

In this unit, you learned the basics of HTML and learned about the new features and advantages of **HTML5**. You learned about HTML **syntax** and important authoring guidelines. You also learned how to declare a document as HTML5, create a basic structure, and define **headings** and **paragraphs**.

Unit 2

In this unit, you learned how to define a document structure by using **semantically meaningful elements**, including <header>, <section>, <nav>, and <footer>. You also learned how to create **lists** and apply **phrase elements**, including <em>, <strong>, <mark>, and <cite>. You then learned how to add **character entities** and apply **attributes**, including the lang, id, and class attributes. Finally, you learned how to define quotes and their sources.

Unit 3

In this unit, you learned how to use **style sheets** to format HTML content. You learned how to embed a style sheet in a document, and how to create an external style sheet and link documents to it. You also learned how to apply **color** and background color, apply basic text and **font styles**, and apply **margins**, borders, and padding. You then learned how to create **rounded corners** and shadows, control element dimensions, create both **fixed** and **flexible widths**, and apply styles to element IDs.

Unit 4

In this unit, you learned how to create and modify **tables** to display tabular data. You learned how to define a **table structure** by using the <thead>, <tbody>, and <tfoot> elements, and you learned how to **apply styles** to table elements. Finally, you learned how to **span** rows and columns to arrange data, headers, and footers.

Unit 5

In this unit, you learned how to create **links**, apply styles to **link states**, and apply styles **contextually**. You also learned about the differences between the GIF, JPG, and PNG **image formats**. You learned how to embed an image, specify image dimensions, and write effective **text alternatives** for embedded images. Finally, you learned how to apply **background images** from a style sheet.

Topic B: Continued learning after class

It is impossible to learn any subject completely in a single day. To get the most out of this class, you should begin applying your new skills and knowledge as soon as possible. We also offer resources for continued learning.

Next courses in this series

This is the first course in this series. The next course in this series is:

- *HTML5: Advanced*

Other resources

For more information, visit www.axzopress.com.

Glossary

Absolute path
A complete URL (address) for a resource.

Attribute
Information that defines a specific characteristic of an HTML element.

Block element
An element that occupies the full width available and creates a new line before and after the element.

Character entities
Codes that represent symbols that are not accessible on standard keyboards.

Class
A global attribute that you can use to classify elements. A class name can be shared among multiple elements in a document.

Contextual selectors
Style selectors that target only those elements that are used in a particular context in the document.

CSS
Cascading Style Sheets, the standard style language of the Web.

Descriptive text
A text alternative that describes the content of an embedded image.

DOCTYPE declaration
A statement that defines the variant of HTML or XHTML in use in a given document.

Embedded style sheet
A style container that is defined by the <style> element, is inserted in a page's <head> section, and influences only that individual page.

Empty tags
HTML elements that do not have closing tags, such as <link> and <img>.

External style sheet
A text file that is saved with a .css extension and contains only CSS style rules.

GIF
Graphic Interchange Format, an image format best used for non-photographic images that have areas of solid color.

Hexadecimal values
Codes that represent the various combinations of red, green, and blue that make up more than 16 million colors.

HTML
Hypertext Markup Language, the standard markup language of the Web.

ID
A unique identifier that is applied to an element by using the id attribute.

Inline element
An element that occupies only the space it requires and does not create new lines before or after the element. Also called a *phrase element*.

Instructive text
A text alternative to an embedded image; this text clearly indicates an action that the user should or can take.

JPG
Joint Photographic Experts Group, an image format optimized for photographic images that contain many colors.

Link states
The four user-defined conditions of a link: link (the default state), hover, active, and visited.

Margin
The space around an element's box.

Nesting
The parent-child relationships of elements in a document structure. Child elements are said to be "nested" inside their parent element.

Ordered list
A list used to display items of information that follow a specific sequence.

Padding
The space between an element's content and its border (the boundary of its box).

Properties
CSS keywords that take specific formatting actions on an element.

Relative path
The address of an external resource relative to the page being viewed.

Replacement text

A text alternative to an embedded image; this text duplicates the text content of an image so that screen readers and other devices can access the information.

Row groups

Table structures defined by any of these three elements: `<thead>`, `<tbody>`, and `<tfoot>`.

Sans serif

A style of font that does not have flourishes (decorations) at the ends of the lines that make up its characters.

Serif

A style of font that has flourishes (decorations) at the ends of the lines that make up its characters.

Unordered list

A list used to display items of information that do not require or imply a specific sequence.

URL

Uniform Resource Locator; a Web address.

Index

G

H

I

J

L

M

N

O

P

Q

R

S

T

U

W